ON

MOORE

S. Jack Odell
The University of Maryland

WADSWORTH

THOMSON LEARNING

Australia • Canada • Mexico • Singapore • Spain
United Kingdom • United States

This book is dedicated to my wife and fellow adventurer,
Barbara Reed Bradford

I wish to thank my wife Barbara Bradford for her many suggestions as
to how to improve and clarify my presentation of Moore's life and
philosophy, and for her tireless editing of my manuscript. I also want
to thank the series editor, Daniel Kolak for his encouragement.

Printed in the United States of America
1 2 3 4 5 6 7 04 03 02 01 00

For permission to use material from this text, contact us:
Web: http://www.thomsonrights.com
Fax: 1-800-730-2215
Phone: 1-800-730-2214

For more information, contact:
Wadsworth/Thomson Learning, Inc.
10 Davis Drive
Belmont, CA 94002-3098
USA
http://www.wadsworth.com

ISBN: 0-534-57630-3

Contents

Introduction

G. E. Moore was one of the most respected and influential philosophers in England during the first half of the 20th Century. He influenced both Wittgenstein and Russell, two of this century's most important philosophers. With Russell, he laid the foundation for analytical philosophy, and he was, in fact, one of the very few philosophers Wittgenstein, who many philosophers consider to be one of the most important philosophers of all time, ever listened to. When Moore was on his deathbed, during his final hours, Wittgenstein would, to the chagrin of Moore's wife Dorothy, push his way into Moore's bedroom, and engage him in philosophical dialogue.[1]

Wittgenstein's final philosophical efforts, posthumously published as *On Certainty*, were inspired by Moore's efforts concerning certainty. He also had a profound influence on the philosophical study of ethics. His work in ethics generated a great deal of philosophical effort on the part of both his critics and his defenders. His inspiration and influence was not restricted to those who pursue philosophy, however. He had a great deal of influence upon that group of thinkers and artists collectively referred to as the "Bloomsbury Group,"[2] among whose most influential members were: Virginia Woolf, John Maynard Keyes, Clive Bell, Desmond MacCarthy, and Lytton Stachey. Virginia Woolf admired him enough to include him in her first novel, *The Voyage Out*. John Maynard Keyes, the great economist, said of Moore's work "it was exciting, exhilarating, the beginning of a new renaissance, the opening of a new heaven on a new earth."[3]

As great as his influence and fame was during his life, few philosophers today read Moore, and many have little knowledge of how significant his influence has been on the course that philosophy took in the Twentieth Century. And, unfortunately, many of those who do read Moore today fail to appreciate his work. Many readers find his style off-putting, and unfairly judge him to be a philosopher who offers much ado about nothing. In order to appreciate his work one has to be willing to plow through seemingly endless details, many of which are dispensable, to get to the gold. His work has to be mined. There is always a mother load there somewhere if one is patient and persistent enough to find it.

Moore is easily distracted. If he recognizes a distinction, he will mark it. He will stake claim to it. This can prove very distracting to the reader, especially when he eventually discovers where Moore has been leading him. The route seems so rococo, so unnecessarily embellished. Given the choice of gaining one's objective via the shortest and quickest means possible, in opposition to a journey through a complicated maze, most would quickly and gladly choose the former path.

Painters like Hals, Goya, and Van Gogh will gloss over and ignore details of background to force us to focus on the central message of their paintings. Vermeer, Holbein, or Durer, on the other hand, are also storytellers, but they cannot resist including an immense number of details surrounding the principal subject matter of their respective works. Moore shares their enthusiasm for detail. Unfortunately, his medium does not allow one the same freedom as that found in the visual arts.

When we view a painting, our own interests will tend to filter out details that are of little or no importance to us. This rarely happens for a reader, especially one unaccustomed to a detailer like Moore. More often than not the reader will simply turn away from such detailers, and turn to philosophers whose prose moves more smoothly from one theme to another. One who reads Moore must be willing to take a stroll through a given theme. He is like a guide who takes us on a walk through Paris, through its museums, around its architecture, to its famous sites, over its boulevards, and in and out of its alleys. At the conclusion of such a tour one may feel that he knows more about Paris than he ever wished to know. Its alleys, while interesting are, for such a tourist, one who wants to see the Louvre, Notre Dame, the Opera House, etc., simply an annoying distraction. Moore seems at times to be a man who has lost his way. Norman Malcolm reports that Wittgenstein once said that he did not believe that Moore would *recognize* a *correct* solution if he were presented with one."[4]

Yet Wittgenstein is also reported by Malcolm to have said both that "what Moore primarily did, as a philosopher, 'was to destroy premature solutions' of philosophical problems," and that "if one were trying to find the right words to express a fine distinction of thought, Moore was absolutely the best person to consult."[5] The reader who remains persistent and patient when reading Moore is often rewarded with a significant and important insight.

Moore was a man on a mission. His mission was to weed out the pompous, pretentious, muddled, and ill-founded theories and theses of philosophy's history. He wanted to replace the vague, and uncertain notions or concepts of philosophy with ones that were clear and certain. He was like a knight, always ready to do battle with those past and present champions of the murky and misleading. His weapon, his Excalibur, was analysis—forged in England by himself and Bertrand Russell, with help from the Germanic philosophers, Frege and Wittgenstein. This method, which would attract other champions in Rudolph Carnap, Gilbert Ryle, A.J. Ayer, Willard Quine, P. F. Strawson, and J. L Austin, and which would eventually split into two factions, was for Moore, as well as these others, a weapon of immense and unpredictable power. It was primarily a method for determining exactness of meaning. For far too long philosophers had misled themselves and others. The reason for this being that the meanings of their principles and doctrines were ambiguous and therefore easily misinterpreted. The fallacy of *equivocation* was present in the works of even the greatest of philosophers, and it was, for the champions of analysis, their perceived and practiced duty to isolate and reveal its many occurrences.

The fallacy of equivocation occurs whenever a word is used in a premise of an argument with a *meaning* different from the *meaning* it would have to have to warrant the argument's conclusion. In such a fallacy a word or expression shifts its meaning in the course of an argument, and this shift in meaning is what makes the argument appear persuasive. For example, "Since good steaks are rare, it follows that they must be hard to find." Moore was a master at ferreting out and revealing this kind of fallacy. His refutation of skepticism consists in his alleging that skepticism is primarily based upon an equivocation on the word 'possible.' I will discuss this at length in Chapter V.

The two factions which practitioners of the analytic method split into came to be known as *logical* analysts on the one hand, and *ordinary language* analysts on the other. Russell, Frege, the early Wittgenstein, and Carnap were perpetuators of the former, whereas the later Wittgenstein, Ryle, and J.L. Austin were the designers of the latter method. Moore and Wittgenstein are the only ones who were instrumental in the development of both forms, though Wittgenstein was far more important in the development of ordinary language philosophy than was Moore.

Not only did Moore contribute most significantly to the development of the analytical method in philosophy, he made important and influential contributions to most of the topics which philosophers commonly address. His critiques of idealism, skepticism, and various ethical theories are among his most successful endeavors. But, on the positive side, he made significant contributions towards our understanding of ethics, perception, certainty, and the nature of existence.

I will begin this book with a chapter on Moore's life and character. In Chapter II, I will examine his views regarding the nature of philosophy and his conception of philosophical analysis. In Chapter III, I will explain his devotion to, and explication of, the concept of "sense-data." I will devote Chapter IV to an explanation of Moore's "refutation" of Idealism, and Chapter V to his "refutation" of skepticism. Chapter VI will address his "defense" of common sense. Chapter VII will examine his position regarding "certainty," and its influence upon Wittgenstein, as well as Wittgenstein's efforts to refute Moore. In Chapter VIII, the final Chapter of this work, I will examine his contributions to ethics.

---

[1] See Norman Malcolm (1962) p.67.

[2] Bloomsbury was the name an unfashionable section of early twentieth century London, where intellectuals could find cheap housing, but the term came to stand for a group of writers and artists who met there at that time, and who championed meritocracy, scholarship, liberalism, and progressive ideas concerning government and education.

[3] For a detailed account of Moore's influence upon this group see Regan (1986).

[4] Malcolm (1962) p. 66.

[5] Ibid., pp. 66-67.

4

1

MOORE'S LIFE AND CHARACTER

Moore's life was very different from that of his friend and colleague, Bertrand Russell. Russell's lifestyle was adventurous, exciting, controversial, political, and sensual. Moore's was none of these things. No one has summed up Moore's lifestyle better than his friend and colleague, C. D. Broad:

> Fundamentally he was a man of simple tastes and character, absolutely devoid of all affectation, pose, and flummery. He thoroughly enjoyed the simple human pleasures of eating and drinking, walking, gardening, talking to his friends, playing with his children, and so on. It is because ordinary, unpretending Englishmen are so often muddle-headed, and intellectuals so often cracked and conceited, that Moore, who combined the virtues of both and had the vices of neither, was so exceptional and lovable a personality.[1]

Here, as well as in nearly every statement about him by those who knew him well, mention is made of his character. It is impossible to find, at least I have not found, anyone who faults Moore's character. He is a philosopher of simple tastes as much respected for his character as for his philosophical acumen. Anyone acquainted the history of philosophy cannot help comparing him to Epicurus. Both philosophers lived simple, unpretentious, and tranquil lives, in the company of

5

friends, in the pursuit of philosophical truth, and none of their associates ever spoke badly of either man. Such men are very rare. An example meant to reveal Moore's unpretentious and genuinely incorruptible nature is an incident related to us by Norman Malcolm:

> The address that Moore delivered to the British Academy, entitled 'Proof of an External World,' caused him a great deal of torment in its preparation. He worked hard at it, but the concluding portion displeased him, and he could not get it right as the time approached for his appearance before the Academy. On the day of the lecture he was still distressed about the ending of the paper. As he was about to leave the house to take the train to London, Mrs. Moore said, in order to comfort him, "Cheer up! I'm sure they will like it." To which Moore made this emphatic reply: "If they *do*, they'll be *wrong!*"[2]

One might, however, be tempted to interpret this incident in a way less complimentary to Moore. It would not be altogether unreasonable to view this incident as evidence that Moore either lacked self-esteem, or was given to false modesty. But this interpretation can be seen to be implausible on the basis of a couple of other anecdotes, which Malcolm also relates. First, there is the following one:

> I recall that once when lecturing before a small class he had occasion to refer to an article that he had published some years before, and he went on to remark, without embarrassment, that it was a *good* article. I was much struck by this. Most men would be prevented by false modesty from saying a thing of this sort in public. Moore's modesty was so genuine that he could say it without any implication of self-satisfaction.[3]

Second, there is my personal favorite, which concerns what happened when Moore was awarded the Order of Merit—the highest honor a man of letters can receive in the British Empire. King George VI made the presentation of this honor to Moore in a private audience. Mrs. Moore waited outside in a cab, and when Moore returned to her at the end of his audience with the King, the first thing he said to his wife was, according to Malcolm, "Do you know that the King never heard of *Wittgenstein!*" Malcolm claims that:

> This exclamation of Moore's illustrates not only his naïveté, but also his complete preoccupation with philosophy. Here is

philosophy, the most exciting thing in the world; here is Wittgenstein, the most exciting figure in philosophy; and here is the King, who had not even heard of Wittgenstein![4]

While I agree with Malcolm's assessment of this incident, I am much more impressed by what it reveals about Moore's remarkable absence of vanity or false modesty than I am with its implications regarding his naïveté and his preoccupation with philosophy. How many human beings could resist, especially in the sole presence of someone as close as one's own spouse, a self-indulgent burst of ego— "The King said I should be extremely proud of my accomplishments," or some such self-aggrandizing comment? No one with whom I have ever been personally acquainted could have resisted this temptation, nor could I.

Although Moore's character sets him apart from others, it is by no means his only distinguishing trait. His relentless pursuit of the truth, and his enormous analytical skills are as distinctive and unique as any of his other characteristics. Again, it is C. D. Broad to whom I shall turn for perspicuous remarks on this aspect of Moore's talent :

> It is doubtful that any philosopher known to history has excelled or even equaled Moore in sheer power of analyzing problems, detecting and exposing fallacies and ambiguities, and formulating and working out alternative possibilities. He knew his own limitations, and within the field of absolutely fundamental problems to which he confined himself, he illuminated and transformed every subject which he treated...Apart from his immense analytic power Moore's most noticeable characteristic was his absolutely single-minded desire to discover truth and avoid error and confusion.[5]

George Edward Moore was born on 1873 in a suburb of London called Upper Norwood. He was the fifth of eight children born to his parents D. Moore, and Henrietta Sturge. He died on October 24, 1958. His family was well connected. They were among those families comprising the so-called "meritocracy," families from, according to Paul Levy, "three distinct groups, those with philanthropic, Quaker or evangelical traditions," which "as a group were to influence profoundly the cultural life of the country." Moreover, according to Levy:

> When the affairs of government and empire became too complicated to be run by the aristocratic ruling class with

7

its traditions of public service, 'members of these intellectual families became the new professional civil servants,' Indian and colonial service officials, headmasters, school inspectors, museum curators, editors and journalists. 'Thus' Lord Annan suggests, 'they gradually spread over the length and breadth of English intellectual life criticizing the assumptions of the ruling class above them and forming the opinions of the upper middle class to which they belonged.[6]

Moore's mother's family, the Sturges, were among the more influential families making up this group, and were quite wealthy. Moore's uncle George Sturge, the richest of the Sturges, bequeathed considerable funds to Moore's family, and it was these funds that made it possible for Moore to pursue his research in philosophy when he was unemployed as a philosophy professor during the years between 1904 and 1911.

Moore's early schooling took place at the day school of Dulwich College. He excelled not only in academic subjects, but in athletic ones as well. He is reputed to have been quite a good footballer. At this school his good fortune was to have been taught by several outstanding teachers, about whom Moore was lavish in his praise. About his years at Dulwich Moore has this to say, "On the whole, I enjoyed my life at school, and was very well satisfied with it; and I left Dulwich with a strong affection both for the school as a whole, and for very many people in it."[7]

One event which occurred while he was at Dulwich and which was the source of some embarrassment for him throughout his life, was his having joined an evangelical Christian youth group. This is one of the very few incidents from this period in his life which he choose to relate in his "Autobiography" for the Schlipp volume on his philosophy. After his conversion, he felt obliged to convert others just as the young members of this group had converted him. He claims to have felt great chagrin at the very prospect of trying to convert his schoolmates at Dulwich, and this made him feel guilty. He felt that his moral character must have been lacking.

Moore's intense religious phase lasted for only a couple of years, and was eventually, because of the influence of his oldest brother, the poet Thomas Sturge Moore, replaced long before he left school by "complete Agnosticism."[8] Although he remained throughout the rest of his life an agnostic, he did express some very interesting views about mankind's religious sentiments. In an essay entitled "Art, Morals, and Religion,"[9] which was written for presentation to the Sunday Essay

8

Society, he argued that Religion is merely a subdivision of Art—that both aim at knowledge of intrinsic Goodness. In essence, Art, for Moore, replaced the conventional religion of his youth. The pursuit of beauty replaced the worship of God. He realized that the pursuit of art is intellectually superior to religion, and its object, beauty, is, unlike God, indisputably attainable. Humans can, on Moore's vision of the nature of things, by their efforts create beautiful things, and thereby enrich the world.[10]

Moore spent the greater part of his life in and around Cambridge, England. He attended Cambridge University both as an undergraduate and as a graduate student, and eventually became a chaired Professor of Philosophy. Few, if any, philosophers have ever been more closely tied to one institution than was Moore to Cambridge. It was here that he met those men who would play by far the most important roles in his philosophical development, namely, Sidgwick, McTaggart, Russell, and Wittgenstein. The first two were among his tutors; Russell was his colleague, and Wittgenstein his "pupil." It was here that he became acquainted with those men who would become his best and most enduring friends. Among these men, one needs to mention Robert Trevelyan, the brothers Crompton and Theodore Llewelyn Davies, Roger Fry, Lytton Strachey, and John Maynard Keynes. It was Fry, Strachey, and Keyes, among the most influential members of the "Bloomsbury," who were in large part responsible for Moore's participation in and influence of the course taken by that group of artists and thinkers. It was at Cambridge that his teachings and philosophical ideas took root, and from which they were spread throughout the world. It was at Cambridge that he died, October 24, 1958.

Moore entered Trinity College, Cambridge in 1892. He was a distinguished student, receiving a First both in Classics and in Moral Science. In 1898 he was awarded a prize-fellowship at Trinity College, which he held until he left Cambridge in 1904. He returned to Cambridge in 1911, and taught philosophy there for twenty-eight years, until 1939, at which time he was forced by University Statutes to retire. However, he remained on as a Fellow of Trinity College—to which any Fellow who has completed his term of service is entitled for life.

As an undergraduate at Cambridge Moore was elected to an elitist secret society, the Cambridge Conversazione Society, known as "The Apostles." It had been founded in 1820 by George Tomlinson, and at its inception was not secret. In its ranks are to be found some of the most distinguished graduates of Cambridge, including: Alfred (Lord) Tennyson, Henry Sidgwick, Rupert Brooke, John Maynard Keyes,

Bertrand Russell, Alfred North Whitehead, J. Ellis McTaggart, and Ludwig Wittgenstein (who resigned shortly after election). The society blundered occasionally and passed over some very worthy candidates, the most notable of which was Charles Darwin.

The Society of Apostles carried out its business in strict accordance with its rites and rituals. Every member of the Apostles was required to serve on occasion as "moderator" and read a paper to the other Apostles, and it had to be read from the "hearth rug." When the moderator finished reading his paper, lots were drawn to determine the order of the questioning. Election to the society was for life, and every member was required to attend every meeting while in residence at Cambridge, though there was a procedure in place for excusing one from attendance.

Moore was evidently quite delighted with being a member of this society, and always ready to serve as moderator. His election was assured when he impressed McTaggart, who was, at that time, one of Cambridge's premier philosophers. It was Bertrand Russell who first recognized that Moore had considerable intellectual talent, enough talent to become an important philosopher. He arranged for a meeting, a tea, between Moore and McTaggart in his own rooms at Cambridge. Moore's recollection of this meeting has become an often-recounted example of Moore's reluctance to be impressed, even in the most auspicious of circumstances. The story Moore relates is that McTaggart launched his infamous hypothesis that time was unreal, which Moore regarded as a perfectly "monstrous proposition," and which he claims to have argued persistently against, finding "quite a lot of different things to say in answer to McTaggart."[11] At any rate, whatever he said must have impressed McTaggart, because, although it was Russell who proposed Moore for membership in the Apostles, it was McTaggart's vote that clinched it for Moore. Moore's initial performance, as well as most of his subsequent performances as an Apostle did not disappoint. Russell and others have testified to the excellence and sometimes-electrifying quality of Moore's contributions to the Society.[12]

While on Fellowship at Cambridge (1898-1904) Moore published many of his most important and influential works: "The Nature of Judgment" (1899), *Principia Ethica* (1903), and "The Refutation of Idealism" (1903). The first mentioned essay led to the development of the analytic method in philosophy, the second mentioned work was for a long time considered to be one the most important works ever written on the subject of ethics. It is still held in high regard today. The last mentioned work was written at a time when Idealism was at its zenith in England as well as in Germany. It was championed at that time by both F. H. Bradley and J. Ellis McTaggart, who were the philosopher kings at Cambridge court. Moore's attack on Idealism was direct and difficult to repel. Idealism was reeling from Moore's attack when Russell and Wittgenstein, inspired by Moore's analytic method, rushed in to nearly finish it off. I say, "nearly finish it off" because it was able to retaliate against the positivist's flawed, but Wittgenstein inspired, attempts to expunge it.

During Moore's seven-year sojourn away from Cambridge, he spent the first half living in Edinburgh, Scotland, and the second half living in London. According to Moore, he spent part of his time in Edinburgh "trying to understand Russell's *Principles of Mathematics*," an effort which eventually resulted in his publishing a long review of this work. In London, he was invited to give two courses of ten lectures each at Morley College on the subject of Metaphysics. Toward the end of his stay in London he wrote a small book entitled *Ethics*, which he "liked better than *Principia Ethica*."[13]

In 1911 Moore was asked to return, and did return, to Cambridge as a Lecturer in Moral Science. In fact, he claimed to have "jumped" at the offer. He began at this time a succession of lectures lasting for twenty-eight years. He lectured every term during this twenty-eight year period. And he produced several extremely important and influential works: "The Status of Sense-Data" (1914), "A Defense of Common Sense" (1925), and "Proof of an External World" (1939). The first work legitimized to some extent the existence of sense-data. The last two had considerable impact on the last work of Wittgenstein, *On Certainty*.

No account of Moore's life and philosophy would be complete without a discussion of his impact upon that group know as the Bloomsbury. As I pointed out in my introductory chapter, Moore's influence upon that group of thinkers and artists was considerable. Virginia Woolf, John Maynard Keyes, Clive Bell, Desmond MacCarthy, and Lytton Stachey were all members of this group. I also pointed out in the introduction that Virginia Woolf admired him enough to include him in her first novel, *The Voyage Out*, and that John Maynard Keyes said of Moore's work that "it was exciting, exhilarating, the beginning of a new renaissance, the opening of a new heaven on a new earth." He also said of the chapter on the Ideal in Moore's *Principia Ethica* "there is nothing like that chapter in all literature since Plato." And, surprisingly—astonishingly to some—he adds, "it is better than Plato."[14] Lytton Strachey said in a letter to Moore (in Moore's Papers) that he was of the opinion that Moore's

Principia "has not only wrecked and shattered all writers on Ethics from Aristotle and Christ to Herbert Spencer and Mr. Bradley, it has not only laid the true foundations of Ethics," it has led to the "establishment of that Method which shines like a sword between the lines. It is the scientific method, deliberately applied, for the first time to reasoning."

There can be no doubt that Moore was an immense influence upon the Bloomsbury group. Whether or not they understood what he was saying is another question. It has been argued by more than one author that they did not—that they simply interpreted his writings to say what they wanted them to say. They constructed their own Manifesto, and praised him for it.[15] Be that as it may, it is now time to let go of Moore's life and turn to his philosophy.

---

[1] Broad (1958) p. 12.
[2] Malcolm (1963) p. 166.
[3] Ibid., p. 163.
[4] Ibid., p. 166.
[5] Broad (1958) p. 12.
[6] Levy (1981) p. 19.
[7] Schilpp (1952) p. 10.
[8] Ibid., p.11.
[9] Moore (Between 1895-1901).
[10] For a more extensive account of Moore's views on the matter of religion see Regan (1986) pp. 153-182.
[11] Schilpp (1952) pp. 13-14.
[12] See Levy (1981) for a detailed account of Moore as an Apostle. pp. 123-167.
[13] Ibid., pp. 25-27.
[14] Keynes (1949) p. 94.
[15] For a detailed account of this matter see Regan (1986).

2

The Nature of Philosophy and The Analytic Method

Moore attempts to answer the meta-philosophical question, "What is Philosophy?" in terms of the kinds of problems it raises. He devotes the first chapter of his book *Some Main Problems of Philosophy* to answering this question. According to Moore, "the first and most important problem of philosophy" is to "give a general description of the whole universe." This problem is, according to Moore, "peculiar to philosophy," for "there is no other science which tries to say" that certain "kinds of things are the *only* kinds of things that there are in the Universe, or which we know to be in it." Although he claims that there is no other science or discipline that attempts to give a description of the entire universe, Moore recognizes that "there are certain views about the nature of the Universe, which are held, now-a-days, by almost everybody." These universally held views Moore labels the "Common Sense view."[1]

Moore then proceeds to characterize philosophy by pointing out that the "most amazing and most interesting" thing about the views of many philosophers is that they are in complete disagreement with Common Sense. Philosophers "profess to know that there are in the Universe most important kinds of things, which Common Sense does not profess to know of, and also they profess to know that there are *not* in the Universe (or, at least, that, if there are, we do not know it), things of which Common Sense is most sure."[2]

Moore goes on to characterize the Common Sense view of the Universe, which he summarizes as follows:

> Firstly, that there certainly are in the Universe two very different kinds of things, namely material objects and acts of consciousness. And secondly, as to the relation of these two kinds of things three points: the first (1) that conscious acts are attached to comparatively few among the material objects in the Universe; that the vast majority of material objects are unconscious...(2) that material objects are all of such a kind that they may exist, even when we are not conscious of them, and that many do in fact so exist...(3) that there *may* have been a time when acts of consciousness were attached to *no* material bodies anywhere in the Universe, and *may* again be such a time; and that there almost certainly was a time when there were no human bodies, with human consciousness attached to them, upon this earth.[3]

He adds two "other points," which I shall refer to as (4) and (5), and will in part paraphrase as:

> (4) That all material objects, and all acts of consciousness of ourselves and other animals upon the earth are in *time*. (5) That we know (1), (2), (3) and (4) to be true—that we also know an immense number of details about particular material objects and act of consciousness, past, present, and future.[4]

Moore proceeds by asserting that "a great class of subordinate philosophical problems" consists "in trying to define more clearly the various kinds of things that philosophers posit as existing and non-existing, in order to distinguish clearly between, for example, mind and body, God and man." He then assigns all those issues concerning the ultimate constituents of the universe to "that department (he uses the expressions 'branch' and 'department,' interchangeably) of philosophy which is called Metaphysics."[5]   He then turns to another set of problems characteristic of philosophy—problems which have "an evident bearing on that problem that characterizes Metaphysics, namely, the problem concerning the general description of the universe." This second problem characteristic of philosophical concern is the knowledge or epistemological problem, "How do we know, and what are the limits of human knowledge?" According to Moore, "a large part of philosophy has, in fact, consisted in trying to classify completely all the different ways in which we can *know* things; or in trying to describe exactly particular ways of knowing them." Moore assigns this problem to that branch of philosophy known as logic (today it is common to refer to this branch with the term 'epistemology').[6]

The third problem characteristic of philosophy is, Moore contends, the problem concerning the nature of the good, or the problem of ethics. On Moore's account of ethics, it attempts "to classify all the different sorts of things which *would* be good or bad, right or wrong, in such a way as to be able to say: Nothing would be good unless it had certain characteristics, or one or the other of certain characteristics." And nothing would, on Moore's account, be bad, unless the same kind of thing were true of it, and accordingly for right and wrong.[7]

Moore's final observation about philosophy is that ethics and metaphysics are in two ways importantly connected. In the first place it is of the utmost importance to recognize the fact that there is within the universe "these distinctions of good and bad, right and wrong." And second, "by combining the results of Ethics as to what *would* be good or bad, with the conclusions of Metaphysics as to what kinds of things there are in the universe" we can answer the question concerning whether the "Universe is, on the whole, good or bad."[8]

Interestingly, although Moore defines philosophy in terms of the positions it takes regarding ethics, epistemology, and metaphysics, Moore himself almost always defends Common Sense against the views of most philosophers. He is primarily critical of philosophy. He rarely speculates or puts forward doctrines about the nature of things. There is one *notable* exception to this generalization, however. He does assert and defend a positive doctrine about the nature of the good, namely that it is a non-natural property that some things have and others lack. We will return to this doctrine in a later chapter.

Moore can without exaggeration be credited with having provided the foundation for the analytic movement in philosophy. His 1899 article for *Mind*, "The Nature of Judgment," which Russell regarded as Moore's most significant philosophical work, stands in evidence of this claim. Nevertheless, it was he and Russell who together *worked out* the details of this approach to philosophy.[9]

For Moore, philosophy, at least good philosophy, was from the beginning synonymous with analysis. And this fact about him sets him apart from most philosophers. Most philosophers are attracted to philosophy because of the so-called "big questions" it attempts to answer, questions like "What is the meaning of human existence?" "What is the nature of the universe, and what is our role in it?" and "Where do we come from, and who or what is responsible for our existence?" These perplexing questions occur to many of us in some form or other in late childhood or sometime during our early teens. Desire on our part to find answers to such questions may very well lead, and in fact often has led, philosophers to their discipline. Not so for Moore. He claims in an often quoted passage from his "Autobiography" for the Schilpp volume on his philosophy that:

> What has suggested philosophical problems to me is things
> which other philosophers have said about the world or the
> sciences. In many problems suggested in this way I have been
> (and still am) very keenly interested—the problems in question
> being mainly of two sorts, namely, first, the problem of trying to
> get really clear as to what on earth a given philosopher *meant* by
> something which he said, and, secondly, the problem of
> discovering what really satisfactory reasons there are for
> supposing that what he meant was true, or, alternatively, was
> false. I think I have been trying to solve problems of this sort all
> of my life...[10]

There is good reason why this passage has been quoted so often. It is one of the most revealing statements concerning his approach to philosophy that Moore ever made on the subject. As we have seen, Moore characterizes philosophy in terms of the problems it attempts to answer—problems: metaphysical, epistemological, and ethical. Yet none of these problems were *the* problems that most interested him. These problems were, of course, tangentially related to the problem that, he confesses, did most interest him, namely, the problem of clarification and analysis of philosophical discourse. He was interested in philosophizing about what other philosophers *meant by* the things they said. His interests were from the beginning different from those of past philosophers. His focus was like the work he inspired in Wittgenstein. It was metaphilosophical—philosophy about philosophy. It provided the impetus needed to establish philosophical analysis. If anything can be said to propel or be the motor of philosophical analysis, it is the desire to clarify and disambiguate the speculations of philosophers, an inevitable result of which is the elimination of the

16

vague and imprecise. The course for philosophy that Moore set in motion spawned: logical atomism, with its emphasis upon clarification through reductive analysis; logical positivism, with its dedication to the elimination of metaphysics; and finally ordinary language philosophy—the philosophy of the later Wittgenstein—with its commitment to the complete restructuring of, if not the elimination of, all previous philosophy. The extent to which Moore's work was foundational to the work of Russell, Wittgenstein and the logical positivists is not widely recognized among many philosophers today. I will attempt to rectify this situation as I continue to explicate Moore's analytical conception of philosophy.

In his book, *G. E. Moore*, Alan White isolates three distinct notions of analysis, and claims that Moore "seemed to have regarded analysis" in all three of these ways. First, there is the *introspection* view of analysis, which attempts to provide the correct analysis or meaning of a given concept, say the concept of "being a brother," by offering what we *think of* when we think the concept of being a brother. White thinks that this is, in fact, Moore's "basic view of analysis," and he argues, quite convincingly, that this view of the matter is altogether implausible.[11] Moore's second conception of analysis, and the one which is of greatest historical importance, is the *division* view of analysis—that to understand a concept, like "being a brother," one has to break it down into its constituent concepts, in the case under consideration, "being male," and "being a sibling." The third conception of analysis that White attributes to Moore is that analysis is *distinction*, which is to say that the meaning of a concept, our example "being a brother," is specified by clarifying how it is "related to and distinguished from other notions which are conveyed either by the same or different expressions." This third notion White, again I think quite rightly, dismisses as being for Moore merely "preliminary" to the task of analyzing a concept.[12] Because the *division* account of analysis is of greatest historical importance, it influenced Russell, Wittgenstein, and the logical positivists, and because I agree with White concerning both the implausibility of the introspection account, and the secondary importance to Moore of the distinction account, I will focus my discussion on the Moore's division account of analysis.

In the Schilpp volume on Moore's philosophy, in his essay "Moore's Notion of Analysis," C. H. Langford distinguished between two kinds of analysis. Given that what is to be analyzed is the *analysandum*, and the analysis of it the *analysans*, these two kinds of analysis are, according to Langford: (1) the analysandum is a verbal

17

expression; (2) the analysandum is either a "concept," "idea," or "proposition." The second of these two kinds of analysis may appear to the reader to be identical with what White referred to as the division notion of analysis, and the first kind may appear to be an as yet undifferentiated notion of analysis. Appearances, however, are deceptive here. The two kinds of analysis distinguished by Langford are actually just two different ways of applying what White has labeled the "division" account of analysis. There is the *linguistic* version of the division account, which answers the question "What is the meaning of the word 'w'?" It can be illustrated by using an example from Carnap's "The Elimination of Metaphysics Through Logical Analysis of Language." Suppose we wish to specify the meaning of the word 'arthropod.' The first step in its analysis is, according to Carnap, to place the expression in question in an elementary sentence form 'x is an arthropod.' Its analysis is then provided as:

(a) x is an animal.
(b) x has jointed legs
(c) x has a segmented body.

According to Carnap, 'x is an arthropod' *means* (a), (b), and (c). There are, however, according to Carnap, three other questions which this way of proceeding answers: (1) what sentences is the elementary sentence, S, deducible from, and what sentences are deducible from it? (2) under what conditions is S supposed to be true, and under what conditions false? (3) how is S to be *verified?*. Carnap prefers (1). He even claims that it is the *correct* formulation. Nonetheless, he claims that it is in this way that the meaning of a word is fixed. The meaning of any "meaningful" word is accordingly fixed by reducing it to other words.[13]

In "A Reply to My Critics," in the Schilpp volume, Moore acknowledges the distinction between these two different versions of the division account of analysis, but disclaims the first version and adopts the second one—the *ontological* version. He says, "When I have talked of analyzing anything, *what* I have talked of analyzing has always been an idea or a concept or proposition, and not a verbal expression."[14] This is *not*, according to Moore, to say that one can give an analysis without making use of verbal expressions. He then provides us with what he considers to be three different but equally proper ways of giving an analysis for the concept "being a brother":

(a) The concept "being a brother" is identical with the concept being a "male sibling."

(b) The propositional function "x is a brother" is identical with the propositional function "x is a male sibling."

(c) To say that a person is a brother is the same thing as to say that that person is a male sibling.[15]

Moore then cautions us against using the word 'means' in providing an analysis because "by using it, you at once imply that the *analysandum* is a *verbal expression*, and therefore give a false impression as to what the assertion is that you really wish to make." This move sets Moore apart from Carnap, who as we have seen thinks it appropriate to describe an analysis as providing the meaning of an elementary sentence containing the expression to be analyzed. The question that Moore's method of analysis answers is, in terms of (a) above, "Given any concept C, what are the elementary concepts to which it can be reduced?" Moore's question does not correspond to any of Carnap's formulations of the basic methodological question that analysis is supposed to answer. Instead, it would attempt to answer the question concerning the concept "arthropod" by reducing it to the concepts of "being an animal," "being a jointed-legged animal," and "being a segmented-bodied animal."

Moore goes on to point out that Langford has argued that all three of the ways he favors for giving the analysis of the concept of 'being a brother' give rise to "the paradox of analysis." Moore illustrates this paradox by use of yet a fourth way of stating the analysis in question, namely, "To be a brother is the same thing as to be a male sibling." He claims:

The paradox arises from the fact that, *if* this statement is true, then it seems as if it must be the case that you would be making exactly the same statement if you said: "To be a brother is the same thing as to be a brother." But it is obvious that these two statements are *not* the same; and obvious also that nobody would say that by asserting "To be a brother is to be a brother" you were giving an analysis of the concept "brother."[16]

Moore confesses that "he cannot give a clear solution" to this puzzle, but that some plain facts have emerged from his discussion of

19

this issue, which are:

    (a) both *analysandum* and *analysans* must be *concepts*, and, if the analysis is a correct one, must, in some sense, be *the same concept*,[17] and (b) that the *expression* used for the *analysandum* must be a different *expression* than that used for the *analysans*... (c) that the *expression* used for the *analysandum* must not only be *different* from that used for the *analysans*, but they must differ in this way, namely, that the expression used for the *analysans* must *explicitly mention* concepts which are not explicitly mentioned by the expression used for the *analysandum*.[18]

For Moore, a proposition is an existing thing, and a thing, which can be analyzed, which is to say that a proposition is a complex object—a synthesis of concepts. This approach, which rejects the linguistic account in favor of the ontological one, was adopted and modified by both Russell and the early Wittgenstein, and it led to the ontological or metaphysical view which they championed—logical atomism—which in turn led to logical positivism, which ironically attempted to eliminate metaphysics. According to Ray Monk, in his recent book on Russell:

    ...for Moore, and even more crucially, for Russell, analysis is not—as is commonly understood now—a linguistic activity, but an ontological one. To analyze a proposition is not to investigate a portion of language, it is not to attend to words, it is, so to speak, to carve up the world so that it begins to make some sort of sense. 'A thing becomes intelligible first', writes Moore, 'when it is analyzed into its constituent concepts.'[19]

Moore's view of analysis as the means for discovering the truth about the world becomes for the early Wittgenstein, the Wittgenstein of the *Tractatus*, the model on which he bases his atomism. For Wittgenstein, complex propositions, the propositions of everyday discourse, must be reduced to propositions about simple objects if we are to eliminate ambiguity. The truth of these *atomic propositions* can be read off of the world of facts—*atomic facts*. The atomic propositions merely *picture* atomic facts. If a proposition cannot be broken down into atomic propositions, it is nonsense. For Wittgenstein, an atomic fact is a fact consisting of a simple object in some relation, which can be a monadic, dyadic, triadic, or *n*-adic relation, respectively, being blue, being to the left of some other simple object, being between two such other simple objects, or standing in some relation involving more than three other such simple objects. But it may be asked what exactly are simple objects?

In his "Elimination of Metaphysics through Logical Analysis of Language" Carnap claimed that the analysis he provided for "x is an arthropod" was subject to further analysis, and that there was serious disagreement among philosophers concerning what would be the final analysis. As we just determined, on Wittgenstein's account of the matter, the analysis would terminate in reference to logical atoms or simples. The same was true for Russell. Just what these simples were was initially left unspecified by both philosophers. They claimed that as logicians their task was not to specify the nature of the simples, but simply to demonstrate that they must exist. The Wittgenstein of the *Tractatus* held on to this opinion. Russell did, however, eventually relent and declare the simples to be sense–data. According to Carnap, however, at least two other possibilities existed. One could claim that the simples are gestalts, like, "red here," and "joy now." The other possibility he considers is that the givens of perception are things; either physical objects like tables, chairs, and dogs or parts thereof.[20]

Moore believed, as Russell did, that all perceptual statements concerning physical objects have to be analyzed in terms of statements about sense-data, but his analysis of the term 'sense-datum' left open the question whether or not they were mental or physical entities. In "A Defense of Common Sense" (1925) about the proposition 'This is a hand,' Moore said that two things seemed to him to be quite certain about its analysis, namely:

(1) there is always some *sense-datum* about which the proposition in question is a proposition—some sense-datum which is *a* subject (and, in a certain sense, the principle or ultimate subject) of the proposition in question.

(2) that, nevertheless, *what* I am knowing or judging or knowing to be true about this sense-datum is not (in general) that it is *itself* a hand...[21]

The way Moore defined the term 'sense-data' made it virtually impossible to doubt that they existed. He used the term to mean what we actually perceive—hear, feel, or taste. No one seriously doubts, not even philosophers, that we do see, hear, feel, and taste various things. He was, however, throughout his career unable to decide exactly what

21

they were, i.e., what sort of thing we *actually* perceive. For Moore, the question just what is it that we actually or ultimately see, hear, etc. was a most unsettling question—a question I shall return to in the next chapter. Before proceeding to that chapter, however, I want to explicate a serious objection to philosophical analysis of the sort Moore inspired, and in which he participated.

Every variation of philosophical analysis that I have considered in this chapter—Moore's version and those he inspired—have been rendered, at the very least, dubious on grounds provided by both William James and the Wittgenstein of the *Investigations*. In the *Varieties of Religious Experience* (1901-1902), William James argued that the word 'religion' "cannot stand for any single principle or essence, but is rather a collective name...let us rather admit freely at the outset that we may very likely find no one essence, but many characters which may alternately be equally important to religion." He argued that the same is true of other terms as well, including "government.'[22] In the *Investigations*, Wittgenstein makes the same point by arguing that many general terms, for example, 'game,' 'good,' and 'knowledge' are governed not by essential properties or characteristics, but by overlapping and crisscrossing similarities or characteristics.[23] According to Wittgenstein, the best "expression to characterize these similarities" is to refer to them as "family resemblances." If James and Wittgenstein are correct then, it is pointless, even senseless, to attempt to provide an analysis of such family resemblance words (concepts for Moore) in terms of essential conditions (for Moore, those other concepts essentially contained in the concept being analyzed).

But, cannot this kind of objection be surmounted by claiming that although many of our everyday words are family resemblance words, they can and should be redefined in terms of sufficient and necessary conditions, and that there would be an obvious advantage to gain from doing so. By redefining our ordinary expressions in terms of necessary and sufficient conditions we eliminate ambiguity and prevent misunderstanding—the *raison d' etre* of philosophical analysis. Wittgenstein's counter to this occurs in paragraph 80 of the *Investigations* when he talks about the disappearing chair. His point of view has been explicated and couched in terms of "open texture" by Frederick Waismann in his paper "Verifiability." Neither Waismann, nor Wittgenstein applied the idea expressed by Waismann as "open texture" precisely as I am about to do in order to meet the challenge I have put before the reader. Take Carnap's example 'arthropod,' the meaning of which he has attempted to fix. Suppose that at some time T^1 the object that I have before me is an animal with a segmented body and jointed legs—an arthropod. Suppose, however, that at T^2 it no longer has a segmented body. Suppose further that at T^3 it once again meets all three of those conditions alleged to be necessary for it to be arthropod. What do we want to say about this object? Was it always an arthropod? Was it one at T^1 and T^3, but not at T^2? Was it not an arthropod at all? Was it an arthropod, but a new species of arthropod? Was it a quasi-arthropod? Who knows? But if its meaning were actually fixed, we would know how to answer all of these questions. Unfortunately, for the kind of analysis under consideration this kind of consideration can be generalized to apply to all empirical terms. No matter how many conditions one stipulates to be necessary for the correct application of any given empirical term, the satisfaction of that set will not provide a set sufficient to fix the meaning of that term. They may all be satisfied at T^1, yet it is logically possible that at some time T^2, one of more of those conditions will be lacking.[24]

---

[1] Moore (1953) pp. 1-2.

[2] Ibid., p.2.

[3] Ibid., pp. 10-11.

[4] Ibid., pp. 11-12.

[5] Ibid., pp. 24-25.

[6] Ibid., pp. 25-26.

[7] Ibid., p. 26.

[8] Ibid., pp. 26-27.

[9] See Monk (1996) pp. 116-119.

[10] Schilpp (1952) p. 14.

[11] White (1958) pp. 66-72.

[12] White (1958) pp. 66-83.

[13] Carnap (1932) pp.62-63.

[14] Schilpp (1952) pp. 661-662.

[15] Ibid., p.664.

[16] Ibid., p.665.

[17] In opposition to Moore, not every word can be said to involve a concept. The word 'concept' has a job to do in our language, but its job description does not include its use as a referent for words like 'dog,' 'cat,' 'hand,' etc. Only philosophers talk about the concepts of "dog," "cats," etc. Dogs and cats inhabit the same world we do. They are not abstractions, and so when we want to

inform someone regarding what kinds of things they are, we can simply point to one of them, or to pictures of them. Not so for words like 'democracy,' 'justice,' 'truth,' etc. Democracy, justice, and truth are abstractions. They *are* concepts.

[18] Schilpp (1952) p. 666.

[19] Monk (1996) p.117.

[20] Carnap (1932) p. 63.

[21] Moore (1959) p. 54.

[22] James (1901-02) p. 27.

[23] Wittgenstein (1958) para. 66-67, p.33^e.

[24] See Odell (1984-A) pp.133-134, & Odell (1984-B) pp. 240- 242.

3

Sense-Data

Few, if any, philosophers have had a more lengthy and intimate relationship with a specific concept than has Moore with the concept of "sense-data." He devoted a long chapter to this topic in his book, *Some Main Problems of Philosophy*. He discussed the nature of sense-data in numerous articles, as well as in lectures, reviews, and in conversations with students and colleagues. They get discussed in essays as divergent in subject matter as his "Refutation of Idealism," "The Nature of Perception," "A Defense of Common Sense," and "Is Existence a Predicate?" The last essay he published, just one year before his death, was, as its title proclaimed, "Visual Sense-Data," concerned with this topic! In each of these essays the notion of sense-data plays a fundamental role. Propositions based on direct perception are always analyzed or reduced to propositions about sense-data.

Moore begins an early essay entitled "The Status of Sense-Data" (originally published in 1913-14) by distinguishing between five different kinds of sensory experiences all of which "consist in the fact that an entity of some kind or other is *experienced*." According to Moore, these are: (1) images, (2) dreams, (3) hallucinations, (4) after images, and (5) sensations proper. The entity which is experienced in each of these cases can be any of the following kind of thing: patches of color, sounds, smells, tastes, images of color patches, images of taste, etc., but we must distinguish, Moore tells us, between the entity which is experienced in each of these kinds of case, and the *experiencing* of it. His distinction is the distinction between act and

25

object, specifically between mental acts and mental objects. He calls the entities or objects of mental acts "sensibles," and announces that the question which his essay is meant to answer is, "What is the status of sensibles?" Given the title of this essay, one expects him to answer the question, "What is the status of sense-data?" Why the switch? According to Moore, the etymology of the term 'sense-datum' suggests something that is *given*, but the entities he wishes to discuss need not actually be given, but are only possible givens. He claims that such divergent phenomena as color patches, sounds and tastes, have some common and intrinsic property that identifies them as sensibles. He argues that sounds and colors and tastes as experienced are in essence sensibles because they all possess this property. This property cannot, however, according to Moore, be analyzed.[1]

Moore's idea that there must exist some specific property, analyzable or not, simply because we call all these things sensibles or sensations is, however, ill founded. Like Wittgenstein's "game example," the words 'sensibles,' 'sensations,' and other similar descriptions are family resemblant in nature. The characteristics that govern the correct use of such terms overlap and crisscross throughout that complex of things, some of which are visual, some auditory, and some tactile.

In *Some Main Problems of Philosophy* Moore defines sense-data in terms of perception. They are treated as what is directly apprehended when we perceive physical objects. Moore expresses conviction that the evidence of the senses provides the basis for our knowledge of material objects. For simplicity's sake, he limits his discussion to visual perception with the proviso that "All the general principles which I point out with regard to the sense of seeing, will, I think, be easily transferable, *mutatis mutandis*, to all the other senses by which we can be said to perceive material objects."[2] Seeing is defined to be the *mental act* of seeing, not what goes on in the eyes, nerves, and the brain. To illustrate what he means by a visual sense-datum Moore asks his audience to look at an envelope he is holding in his hand, and proceeds to describe part of what he experienced when he looked at the envelope. He declares that he "saw a patch of a particular whitish color, having a certain size, and a certain shape...These things: this patch of whitish color, and its size and shape I did actually see...And I propose to call these things....*sense-data.*[3]

In "A Defense of Common Sense" (1925) he attempts to clarify his position regarding the existence and nature of sense-data. He acknowledges that some philosophers have had doubts regarding

26

whether sense-data even exist, but that the way he now proposes to use the term there cannot be the slightest doubt that they exist. He asks the reader to look at his own right hand, and then points out that if the reader does as instructed he will be able to pick out some one thing:

> with regard to which he will see that it is ...a natural view to take that that thing is identical, not, indeed with his whole right hand, but with that part of its surface which he is actually seeing, but will also (on a little reflection) be able to see that it is doubtful whether it can be identical with the part of the surface of his hand in question. Things *of the sort* (in a certain respect) of which this thing is, which he sees in looking at his hand, and with regard to which he can understand how some philosophers should have supposed it to *be* the part of the surface of his hand which he is seeing, while others have supposed that it can't be, are what I mean by 'sense-data'.[4]

Moore appears to be on safe ground with this definition. Any definition that defines what we actually see when we claim to see something with sense-data is even compatible with their being physical objects. But, if it turns out that what one actually sees when he follows Moore's instructions is his own hand, then Moore's use of the term 'sense-data' is pointless or redundant. We would have no need for it. Moore attempts to counter this kind of objection by arguing that it is certain that one does not directly ever see one's own hand, that what one means when one claims to see his hand is that he sees something *representative* of it. His certainty seems to be based upon the *assumption* that one does not see one's own hand unless one sees all of it, and by all of it he means its back as well as its palm, its bones, its skin, its arteries, and its veins.[5] But this assumption is dubious at best. It would force us to redefine 'seeing' as something different from the way we presently define it.

When we claim to see something like a hand, we never *mean* that we see *all* of it. Seeing a hand is not seeing all of its parts. If it were, no one would ever be said to see a hand or any other material object. Nor by parity of reason could one ever be said to have repaired an automobile unless one repaired all of its parts. Moreover, seeing only a part of the surface of a material object is, as far as ordinary parlance is concerned, not what happens when one sees a hand. Seeing part of the surface of a hand is the sort of thing that can only be said to happen

27

when, for example, that is all that remains of the hand one is seeing. A forensic anthropologist will sometimes only examine or look at a part of the surface of a human hand. The distinction between seeing only part of (the surface of) a material object and seeing that object itself would be lost if we were to redefine seeing as only seeing part of an object. What the anthropologist does when he does his job, would be on this account be no different from what any of us do everyday countless times. Moore use of language in the essay under consideration is what Wittgenstein would later describe as language on a holiday! It would not be doing its job.

On the basis of this mistaken assumption that what we actually see in cases like the hand case is at best only part of the hand's surface, Moore infers that there are only three possibilities, none of which he regards as certain, regarding what it is that we actually see when we see a hand—which is to say that sense-data have to be one of these three kinds of thing. Or, to put it still differently, Moore holds that there are *just* three possible ways to analyze the proposition 'This is part of the surface of a human hand,' none of which is "nearly certain." First, they could actually be parts of the surface of the hand—that the relation between sense-data and parts of the surfaces of material objects is one of identity. Second they are not identical to sense-data, but stand in an "ultimate and unanalysable" relation of representation to actual parts of material things. Three, they stand in a complex kind of relation of the sort specified by phenomenalism—material things are just permanent possibilities of sensation. On this account, the claim that one is seeing a hand must be analyzed as claiming that I am at present sensing a variety of sense-data, and if certain conditions obtain, I will sense various other sense-data "intrinsically" related to those I now sense, but should different conditions obtain, I will sense a different but also intrinsically related set of sense-data.[6]

Moore addresses each of these possibilities, and formulates various objections to them. The most serious objection to the first possibility is, according to Moore, the "double image" phenomena. In such cases we "certainly have," says Moore, "*two* sense-data each of which is *of* the surface seen, and which cannot therefore both be identical with it... It looks, therefore, as if every sense-datum is...only 'representative' of the surface of which it is a sense-datum." The second possibility is, according to Moore subject to the "grave objection" that it appears to be impossible to determine how we know that there is one and only one thing (a material hand) which has this ultimate representational relationship to the sense-datum we perceive.

Although Moore concedes that the third alternative might just possibly be true, he, nevertheless, claims that it is "very doubtful" because there are "extremely grave objections" to it. He provides three such objections. One, it cannot be the final analysis since it makes reference to material objects—it claims that "if this material object had been in those positions and conditions." Two, it is doubtful that there is any intrinsic relation between present and possible sense-data. Three, "the sense in which a material surface is 'round' or 'square' would necessarily be utterly different from that in which our sense-data appear to us to be 'round' or 'square.'"[7] His first objection, if I understand it correctly, is simply false. If you examine my formulation of phenomenalism in the previous paragraph you will see that it proceeds from present sense-data to possible sense-data. No mention need be made of material things in the *analysandum*. His second and third objections are obscure and difficult to fathom, particularly the third one. If I understand his second objection correctly, it appears to me to be plausible, but only if one takes it to mean that nothing one presently senses in any way necessitates that one will have a specific sensation in the future. I assume that what he means by his third objection is that those predicates we associate with material objects, for example, "is round," "is square," would have to mean something quite different from what they ordinarily mean when applied to sense-data—they would have to mean not what the present sense-datum reveals, for example, its being round, but also what possible future sense-data would reveal. Understood in this way, his third objection to phenomenalism does seem to me to be a plausible one.

Moore concludes this essay by admitting that although he holds that the proposition which he expresses by the following sentence 'There are and have been material things' "is quite certainly true," no answer which "has been hitherto given" regarding "how this proposition is to be analyzed" is "anywhere near certainly true."[8]

At this point one is apt to lose patience with Moore. One is apt to demand that Moore stop beating about the bush and tell us what sense-data are? Surely, a philosopher who is as certain as Moore is that sense-data exist, must know what they are. As astonishing as it may seem, Moore never made up his mind regarding their nature

In his essay, "A Reply to my Critics," (1942) written after a lifetime of trying to understand the nature of sense-data, he confesses that he cannot make up his mind regarding their nature. While discussing an essay by C. J. Ducasse, critical of his views regarding sense-data, Moore says that "*no* sense-datum can be identical with any physical surface, which is the same as to say that no physical surface can be directly comprehended: that it is a contradiction to say that any is." But then he goes on to reveal that:

> Now at the end of the last section I said that I was strongly inclined to agree with Mr. Bousma, Mr. Murphy and Mr. Marhenke that physical surfaces *are* directly apprehended. I am, therefore, now saying that I am now strongly inclined to take a view incompatible with that which I then said I was strongly inclined to take. And this is the truth. I am strongly inclined to take both of these incompatible views. I am completely puzzled about the matter, and only wish I could see any way of settling it.[9]

His last efforts to clarify his position on the nature of sense-data occurs in his "Addendum to My Reply" (1952), when he responds to an article by A. J. Ayer, which was published after the original publication of the Schilpp volume, and which was critical of what Moore had said in his "A Reply to My Critics." Ayer claimed that Moore should not have had any doubts concerning whether or not what one directly apprehends when one is said to see a table is actually part of the surface of a physical object. Ayer claims that the proposition that some sense-data, in Moore's use of the expression 'sense-data,' (which is to use it to refer to "anything whatever which is *directly apprehended*...whether it be a sound, a smell, a taste, or a visual object of any kind") may possibly be identical with physical entities is false because it is self-contradictory. Moore responds to this charge by reminding the reader that he had in "A Reply to My Critics" admitted that the claim in question *might* be contradictory, but that it is *not obviously* so. Moore claims that Ayer's argument depends upon the truth of three premises, the first two of which he refines so as to avoid their being "obviously false." His refinement concerns the replacement of 'directly perceived' for 'directly apprehended' in these premises. Moore's reason for the substitution is that one could apprehend a sense-datum that another has described to one. But one could not be said to have *directly perceived* it under these circumstances.

It is Ayer's third premise that Moore finds unacceptable. That premise is that "It always makes sense to say of any physical object that it is seen in a sense of the word 'see' from which it does not follow that it exists." Moore points out that the only evidence Ayer supplies in favor of this premise concerns hallucinations. Ayer has argued that Macbeth's question "Is this a dagger which I see before me?" illustrates that use of 'see.' Moore concedes that this would be a case where Macbeth does really see a dagger, but it was not a *real* dagger, and that it would be true to say both (1) he was seeing a dagger and (2) he was not seeing a dagger. But Moore denies that the truth of (1) and (2) would establish the existence of two different senses of the word 'see.' According to Moore, the reason that both (1) and (2) are true is that 'dagger,' not 'see,' is being used in two senses. Moore argues that it is clear that Shakespeare is not representing Macbeth as having seen a physical entity, but rather as having seen an hallucinatory object.[10] According to Moore, Ayer's mistake is that of assuming:

"that because, in saying (1), we are using an expression, namely "was seeing a dagger," which in the immense majority of cases entails "was seeing a physical entity," we must be so using it when we say (1) in the comparatively extremely rare cases of hallucination, only with a different sense of 'see.'[11]

But where does this leave Moore? It leaves him where we found him at the end of his reply to his critics, namely, unable to decide whether the given objects of perception are parts of the surfaces of physical objects, or are mental entities.

[1] Moore (1951) pp. 168-171.
[2] Moore (1953) p. 28-29.
[3] Ibid., p. 30.
[4] Moore (1959) p. 54.
[5] Ibid., p. 54.
[6] Ibid., pp. 55-57.
[7] Ibid., pp. 55-58.
[8] Ibid., pp. 58-59.
[9] Schilpp (1952) p. 658.
[10] Ibid., pp. 682-686.
[11] Ibid., p. 686.

4

Refuting Idealism

Philosophers have long been divided on what constitutes the correct answer to the metaphysical question regarding the ultimate nature of reality. Some, the *dualists*, like Descartes, answer the question by claiming that reality consists of two independent substances: mind and matter. For the dualists, to be is to be either a material or a mental substance. Other philosophers, the *monists*, claim that reality ultimately consists of just one kind of thing. Monists fall into one of two different camps, *materialists* and *idealists*. Materialists, like Epicurus, maintain that the one basic substance is matter. Idealists, like Hegel, argue that the one basic substance is mental or spiritual. *Pluralists*, like Bertrand Russell, claim that there are many different kinds of thing. Today, the major battle is between materialists and non-materialists. Many contemporary philosophers including most cognitive scientists hold the view that mental processes are ultimately nothing more than brain states. When Moore was a student at Cambridge many of his professors were followers of Hegel. Idealism was very much in vogue. The contemporary concern with brain states, computer models, functionalism, etc. was non-existent. Yet some of the moves which have played a significant role in the contemporary controversy concerning whether or not consciousness can be reduced to brain states are relevant to the Idealist/non-idealist debate of a century ago. I will make use of some of these moves towards the end of the present chapter.

Moore's 1903 paper "The Refutation of Idealism" is primarily a refutation of idealism based upon an analysis and rejection of the fundamental principle of idealism, namely, "*esse* is *percipi*"—to be is to be perceived. Moore claims that the thesis of the idealist, that everything is spiritual, implies that the universe has "quite a number of excellent qualities, different from any we commonly attribute to stars or planets or to cups and saucers," and that if he can "refute a single proposition [*esse* is *percipi*] which is a necessary and essential step in all Idealistic arguments, then no matter how good the rest of the arguments may be, I shall have proved that the Idealists have *no reason whatever* for their conclusion."[1] But Moore makes it very clear that his paper has no implications regarding what may actually be the nature of reality. He is simply concerned to show that *esse* is *percipi*—in "all the senses ever given to it"—is false, and thus that no idealist has succeeded in establishing that the universe is spiritual.

Moore begins his analysis of the expression that '*esse* is *percipi*' by announcing that all three of its terms are ambiguous. He first observes that although by '*percipi*' one could mean simply sensation, the Idealists themselves distinguish between 'sensation' and 'thought,' and that they rightly emphasize the latter. On the basis of this observation, he interprets the Idealists to mean by '*percipi*' what we ordinarily mean by the word 'experienced.' The advantage of this interpretation is, according to Moore, that experience is common to both sensation and thought. About the copula or the meaning of 'is,' in the expression '*esse* is *percipi*,' Moore recognizes only three interpretations. One could mean to be asserting that '*esse*' and '*percipi*' are exact synonyms—that they mean the same thing. He immediately concedes that this is *not* what the Idealists mean by the expression in question. This means, according to Moore, that there are only two remaining interpretations to consider. The first of these would treat the 'is' in question as an 'is' of predication, and this would imply "that what is meant by *esse*, though not identical with what is meant by *percipi*, yet includes the latter as part of its meaning."[2] To put the matter in more contemporary terms, what Moore is trying to say is that being perceived is a necessary, though not also a sufficient condition for existing. Moore wrestles with this interpretation, and eventually construes it in a way that he seems to consider to be most favorable to the idealists. According to Moore, *esse* is *percipi* "asserts two distinct terms to be so related that whatever has the one, which I call *esse*, has also the property that it is experienced." Moreover, "it asserts a necessary connexion between esse on the one hand and *percipi* on the other; these two words denoting each a distinct term, and *esse*

33

denoting a term in which that denoted by percipi is not included." This interpretation avoids, according to Moore, the conclusion that what the idealists are maintaining amounts to an empty or barren analytic proposition. Instead, it interprets "*esse* is *percipi*" to be "a *necessary synthetic* proposition," or, in other words, a non-empty, non-trivial, yet necessary truth about the empirical world.[3]

Some continental European philosophers, for example, Husserl, Heideggar, and Brentano, based their philosophy, (phenomenology) on the idea that consciousness is always consciousness *of.* Moore was clearly aware of this fact. In the same year that he published the essay attempting to refute idealism he also published an essay on Brentano. Like the phenomenologists, Moore insists on the distinction between consciousness and its objects, and he utilizes this distinction to refute idealism. Moore argues that the sensation of green is a different sensation than the sensation of blue, yet both are sensations. The common element is an act of sensing. But the objects of consciousness in both mental acts are different. "So that," According to Moore, "if anyone tells us that to say that 'Blue exists' is the same thing as to say that 'Both blue and consciousness exist', he makes a mistake and a self-contradictory mistake."[4] An experience or an awareness of something is one thing. The content of an awareness is something else. An awareness of green and an awareness of blue differ in *content*, though both involve an awareness.

The content of an awareness must, according to Moore, be understood *not* as a property or aspect of an awareness but as its object. According to Moore, "if we never experience anything which is *not* an inseparable aspect of *that* experience, how can we infer that anything whatever, let alone *everything*, is an inseparable aspect of *any* experience?"[5] Having made the distinction between content as an aspect of an experience on the one hand, and as an object of an experience on the other hand Moore argues:

...I think it may be seen that if the object of an Idealist's sensation were, as he supposes, *not* the object but merely the content of that sensation, if, that is to say, it really were an inseparable aspect of his experience, each Idealist could never be aware of himself or any other real thing... when any Idealist thinks he is *aware* of himself or of anyone else, this cannot really be the case. The fact is, on his own theory, that himself and that other person are in reality mere *contents* of an awareness, which is awareness *of* nothing whatever. All that can be said is that there is an

34

awareness in him, *with* a certain content: it can never be true that there is in him a consciousness *of* anything. And similarly he is never aware either of the fact that he exists or that reality is spiritual. The real fact, which he describes in those terms, is that his existence and the spirituality of reality are *contents* of an awareness, which is aware of nothing—certainly not, then, of its own content... And further if everything, of which he thinks he is aware, is in reality merely a content of his own experience he has certainly no *reason* for holding that anything does exist except himself: it will, of course, be possible that other persons do exist; solipsism will not be necessarily true; but he cannot possibly infer from anything he holds that it is not true.[6]

Moore's approach has been criticized by C. J. Ducasse in *The Philosophy of G. E. Moore* (1952). Ducasse maintains that Moore is wrong in his contention that in no case is the *esse* of anything *percipi*. Ducasse maintains that there is "a certain class of cases" in which *percipi* does follow from *esse*. He claims that Moore's contention can be shown to be mistaken if one distinguishes between what is expressed in language between the "cognate accusative and the objective accusative—between, for instance, striking a stroke and striking a man, or waving a farewell and waving a flag."[7] Although Ducasse's argument is highly complex, what he is claiming can be put rather simply. He claims that Moore has failed to appreciate that, for instance, sensing blue is like striking a stroke, or waving a farewell. A sensation of blue is like a bitter or sweet taste, blueness, bitterness, and sweetness cannot be separated from the sensing of them. Ducasse expresses his point thus:

The hypothesis, then, which I present as alternative to Professor Moore's is that "blue," "bitter," "sweet," etc., are names not of objects of experience nor of species of objects of experience but of *species of experience itself*. What this means is perhaps made clearest by saying that to sense blue is then to sense *bluely*, just as to dance the waltz is to dance "waltzily" (i.e., in the manner called "to waltz")... Sensing blue, that is to say, is I hold a species of sensing—a specific variety of the sort of activity generically called "sensing" which, however, (unlike dancing or jumping) is an involuntary and non-motor kind of activity. In this as in all cases where the known is connate with the knowing, what is known by the knowing activity is then *its own determinate nature*

35

on the given occasion.[8]

Moore responds to this criticism of Ducasse in "A Reply to my Critics," which is also contained in Schilpp (1952). He concedes that Ducasse is right and that he was wrong in his paper on Idealism. He agrees with Ducasse that there is a class of cases where *percipi* does follow from *esse*. He even provides an example "a toothache certainly cannot exist without being felt." He points out, however, that both he and Ducasse have used language which would make it difficult for anyone to comprehend what the controversy between them really was. He provides an analysis of some of the key expressions and thereby clarifies their differences. He summarizes his findings thus:

> In that early paper I really was asserting that the *sensible* quality "blue" (and, of course, also should have asserted the same of the *sensible* quality "bitter") *could* exist without being perceived: that there was no contradiction in supposing it to do so. Mr. Ducasse's view is that it *cannot*: that there *is* a contradiction in supposing it to do so. And on *this* issue I am now very much inclined to think that Mr. Ducasse is right and that I in that paper was wrong; my reason being that I am inclined to think that it is as impossible that anything which has the sensible quality "blue," and, more generally, anything whatever which is directly apprehended, any *sense-datum*, that is, should exist unperceived, as it is that a headache should exist unfelt. If this is so, it would follow at once, that *no* sense-datum can be identical with any physical surface... that it is a contradiction to say that any is. [9]

Moore goes on to claim, however, as we saw him claim in the previous chapter on the topic of sense-data, that he is equally strongly inclined to claim otherwise—to claim that parts of physical surfaces can be directly apprehended. And, moreover, as we also saw previously, he confesses to being "completely puzzled" about this matter. He confesses that it would be settled had Ducasse proved that his view was right, but, according to Moore, he has not done so. He rejects Ducasse's *analogy* between seeing blue and striking a stroke, or waving farewell, or dancing a waltz. He grants that when a cricketer makes a particular kind of stroke, his example is a "cut," his making of it is so related to its being a cut that it would be "a contradiction to suppose that a "cut" exists when nobody is making that stroke." The same consideration would apply to waving goodbye and performing a waltz step. He denies, however, that Ducasse has provided any reason to suppose that when one experiences the sensible quality "blue" the existence of the quality "blue" is related to the seeing of it in the same way as is the "cut" related to the making of the stroke—that it would be contradictory to suppose that the quality in question could not exist unless someone were experiencing it.[10]

According to Moore, one cannot see the sensible quality blue without seeing *something* that has that quality. One must see a "blue patch, or a blue line, or a blue spot, etc." "How," asks Moore, "is such an object as this—the sort of object I am calling a "sense-datum"—related to my seeing of it?" Although Moore confesses that he is inclined to think that sense-data cannot possibly exist except when they are directly apprehended, he cannot "see why there should be a contradiction in supposing the opposite."[11] If, for example, sense data are parts of the surfaces of physical objects, then they could exist unperceived. In conclusion, Moore concedes:

> To the solution of *this* problem Mr. Ducasse's solution as to how sensible qualities are related to our experiencing of them does not help me at all. I cannot see that he has given any good reason at all for supposing that the *esse* of sensible qualities is *percipi*, though I believe that there *must* be some good reason.[12]

What are we to conclude from all of this? The answer to this question is that the Moore of 1903 thought that idealism could be refuted by showing that all arguments favoring idealism of which he was aware were *unsound* because all of them involved the false premise that "to be is to be perceived." In 1952, he conceded that he was wrong about the truth of this premise. This does not mean, however, that in 1952 he supported idealism. He did not do so then, nor did he ever do so. Moreover, even if Moore's inclination in 1952 is true, and the being of a sensible quality or sense-datum does entail that it is being perceived, it would not follow that idealism were true. Could any argument prove that Idealism is true? The answer is no, and this point can be demonstrated by focusing upon a mistake which Moore made in the 1903 essay against idealism.

As we saw previously, Moore claims that there are only three ways of understanding the copula in 'esse is percipi.' Moore is wrong about this matter. There is a fourth possibility. In the 1903 essay, "The Refutation of Idealism," Moore was assuming what Russell, Wittgenstein, and other philosophers of that period also assumed—that meaning is reference. This assumption was the foundational principle of Logical Atomism,[13] and it created, as Russell pointed out in his 1905 paper "On Denoting," a number of philosophical paradoxes— paradoxes that he attempted to solve.[14] Although Frege shared with Russell many ideas concerning the nature of language and meaning, he disagreed with him regarding the specifics. For Russell, there are only two kinds of thing to consider namely a sign or symbol and its reference. For Frege, an additional element must be added to this list, namely, a *sinn* or sense. For Frege, there are two kinds of meaning incorporated into the use of every sign, its sense, and its reference. Had Moore taken this ingredient into account, he might have recognized a fourth possibility concerning the copula in '*esse* is *percipi.*' Had he recognized in 1903, that there is a difference between a 'word' or sign, its reference, and its sense, he would, I am convinced, have seen his mistake

At any rate, J.J.C. Smart, a staunch defender of materialism, does make use of Frege's distinction between the sense of an expression and its reference to defend materialism. Whereas, Smart applied Frege's distinction to counter the critics of the materialist's thesis that the mind can be reduced to the material, it can be similarly used to counter the critics of the idealist's reduction of the material to the mental. Frege would interpret the 'is' in question as the 'is' of identity, and treat '*esse* is *percipi*' as he does the sentence, 'The Morning Star is the Evening star,' namely, as establishing a relation between the references of the expressions flanking the 'is,' expressions, however, which differ in meaning (sense for Frege). In other words, although we do mean *different* things when we use the words in question, what we are actually referring to is the *same* thing. In this way, Frege explains both how the 'is' in 'The Morning Star is The Evening Star' can be the 'is' of identity, and how the proposition expressed by the sentence, 'The Morning Star is The Evening Star,' is neither empty and trivial, but is, instead, important and consequential. The discovery that the Morning Star is identical with the Evening Star was one of the most important discoveries in the history of astronomy. Likewise, the idealist can be interpreted to be claiming to have made an equally important discovery. Before it was discovered that the Morning Star and the Evening Star were one and the same planetary body, some ancient astronomer must have ventured the hypothesis that they were identical. How else can one explain the discovery that they are one and the same physical body? This discovery had nothing to do with linguistic meaning. Nothing in the meaning of the two expressions 'The Morning

Star' and "The Evening Star' would ever lead one to such a discovery. The idealists likewise are not claiming to have discovered that the meaning of the expression 'existence' necessarily implies being experienced. They are only claiming that what is referred to by these two terms with different meanings is actually the same thing or same kind of thing, depending upon whether one believes that there is only one mental substance, or many such substances.

There is, however, a significant difference between the idealist's claim that to be is to be perceived, and the claim that The Evening Star is The Morning Star. Anyone who denies the latter claim can be refuted by observational or empirical data. The idealist's claim cannot. In fact, as far as the distinction between sense and reference is concerned, it can, as is evidenced by Smart's use of it, be equally applied in defense of idealism's antithesis, materialism. Since both can be defended by the same ploy, and they are antithetical, neither can be made any more plausible than the other by its use. To establish one thesis over the other, some persuasive argument independent of the distinction between sense and reference will have to be presented. The distinction seems to have relevance only if one fails to see that it can also be used in defense of one's opponent's antithetical position.

I am reminded of an often quoted remark attributed to Frank Ramsey, who was a British philosopher of great promise who died quite young, and who was a contemporary of Moore's. He claimed, and here I am paraphrasing, that whenever a philosophical dispute becomes an irresolvable debate between two alternatives, it is likely that both alternatives are false because they share a common false presupposition. Perhaps, the false assumption that the debate between idealists and materialists is based upon is that there is something to be gained by such a reduction, or that the very controversy makes sense. The latter Wittgenstein, the Wittgenstein of the *Philosophical Investigations*, argued that such controversies are pseudo controversies. For the latter Wittgenstein, philosophy is an ill-conceived discipline that can never succeed because the problems it raises, the questions it poses, cannot because of their very nature be solved, they can only be dissolved.

Whether Wittgenstein is right and those philosophers who attempt, as did Moore, to solve or resolve philosophical problems rather than dissolve them, is a question that should not go unmentioned, but is not a question that can be resolved here.

39

[1] Moore (1951) pp. 2-3.
[2] Ibid., p. 9.
[3] Ibid., pp. 10-11.
[4] Ibid., p. 18.
[5] Ibid., p.28.
[6] Ibid., pp. 28-29.
[7] Schilpp (1952) p. 228.
[8] Ibid., p. 232-233.
[9] Ibid., p. 658.
[10] Ibid., p. 659.
[11] Ibid., p. 660.
[12] Ibid., p. 660.
[13] See Hacker (1996) p. 23, 29-32.
[14] See my *On Russell*, pp. 33-39.

5

Refuting Skepticism

Moore expended considerable time and effort throughout his career defending the views of ordinary people, what he called "common-sense." He was particularly disposed to defend the common-sense view regarding knowledge of the external world—knowledge concerning the existence and characteristics or properties of tables, chairs, dogs, other persons, one's own self, and the past. He even attempted to prove that the external world existed, and as a corollary to refute philosophical skepticism, which is the view that no human being can know with certainty anything whatever about tables, chairs, dogs, other persons, one's own self, or the past. According to the skeptic even if the external world exists, we could never know that it does. His most important works on these interrelated subjects are: "A Defense of Common Sense" (1925), "Proof of an External World" (1939), "Certainty" (1941), and "Four Forms of Scepticism" (1940).[1] In the present chapter I will expound and critically discuss the last mentioned essay. In the next chapter, Chapter VI, I will do likewise for the first two. In Chapter VII, I will explicate Moore's views as expressed in "Certainty." In Chapter VII, I will also bring together most of the material of the present chapter and that of Chapter VI which pertains to the topic of "certainty," and I will present Wittgenstein's critique of Moore's work on that topic. In addition, I will explain and critically discuss what Wittgenstein thought Moore's position should have been. Wittgenstein was inspired to work on the topic of certainty by Norman Malcolm's discussions with him concerning what Moore's views were.

Of the four mentioned essays, all of which concern our knowledge of the external world, Wittgenstein preferred "A Defense of Common

41

Sense," and we will see why he did so in Chapter VII.

Unlike Wittgenstein, I prefer Moore's "Four Forms of Scepticism." In it he very nearly succeeds in putting skepticism to bed. When I first read it, I was convinced that he had actually succeeded in doing so. After some effort on my part, however, I realized that his position was not airtight. It has a small but serious hole. It is, nevertheless, the best possible place to start for anyone interested in understanding what is at stake, and what must be accomplished if one is going to argue in favor of skepticism.

Although Moore's principle target in this essay is the skepticism championed by his friend and colleague Bertrand Russell, what he accomplishes has application to skepticism in general. I will begin by explaining what I take to be the view of the skeptic.

Everyone is skeptical some of the time, but one cannot be branded a skeptic on these grounds. Skepticism is a philosophical thesis. To be a skeptic in the philosophical sense is to maintain that the following principle, SK, is true for at least one class of thing, which is to say that the x in SK can be instantiated for at least one entire class of things.

(SK) No one has ever known or could ever know with certainty anything what-so-ever about things of kind x, not that such things exist, nor that they have any specifiable properties.

Instantiated for physical objects SK becomes:

(SKPO) No one has ever known or could ever know with certainty anything what-so-ever about physical objects, not that such things exist, nor that they have any specifiable properties.

Most philosophical skeptics have been skeptical about more than one kind of thing, and *classical philosophical skeptics* can be said to have instantiated (SK) for all of the following: God, physical objects, other persons, the past, the future, and even the self. Another way of putting the classical skeptic's position is in terms of beliefs:

No one can ever be certain that any of her/his beliefs about God, physical objects, other persons, the past, the future, or his/her self are true.

There is a problem with this *inclusive* formulation, however. Philosophical skepticism is actually more inclusive than this

42

formulation allows for, as there are other classes of things that are included within the skepticism's scope. For reasons that will become clear later, it is best to formulate it in terms of what it excludes from the realm of the uncertain. The *exclusive* formulation of the skeptic's thesis can be stated as follows:

> The only beliefs about which we can be said to be certain are beliefs about momentary sense impressions (sense-data) and those beliefs which Kant has labeled as 'analytic'—those beliefs the meanings of whose predicate terms are contained within the meanings of their subject terms, and whose denials are contradictions.

In "Four Form of Scepticism" Moore considers the various kinds of argument skeptics have used to establish their thesis, specifically those employed by Bertrand Russell in his various writings on the subject: (1) the dream argument; (2) the hallucination argument; (3) the argument from illusion; and (4) the malicious demon argument. Moore claims that (1), (2), and (3) all commit the informal fallacy known as *equivocation.* He takes the philosophical skeptic, specifically Russell, to task for failing to recognize the difference between 'possible for' and 'possible that.' He considers Russell's use of the dream argument to render all our knowledge of the past doubtful, and says:

> What he [Russell] means is roughly: In dreams we often feel as if we were remembering things which in fact never happened. And that we do sometimes, not only in dreams, but also in waking life, feel as if we remembered things which in fact never happened, I fully grant. That this is true I don't feel at all inclined to question. What I do feel inclined to question is that this fact is in any way *incompatible* with the proposition that I do now know for certain that I heard a sound like 'Russell' a little while ago. Suppose I have had experiences which resembled this one in the respect that I felt as if I remembered hearing a certain sound a little while before, while yet it is not true that a little while before I did hear the sound in question. Does that prove that I don't know for certain *now* that I did hear the sound 'Russell' just now? It seems to me that the idea that it does is a mere fallacy, resting partly at least on a confusion between two different uses of the words 'possible' or 'may'.
>
> What really does follow from the premiss is this: That

43

it is *possible for* (the italics are mine) an experience of a sort, of which my present experience is an example, i.e. one which resembles my present experience in a certain respect, *not* to have been preceded within a certain period by the sound 'Russell'. Whereas the conclusion alleged to follow is: It is *possible that* (the italics are again mine) *this* experience was not preceded within that period by the sound 'Russell'. Now in the first of these sentences the meaning of 'possible' is such that the whole sentence means merely: Some experiences of feeling as if one remembered a certain sound are not preceded by the sound in question. But in the conclusion: It is possible that this experience was not preceded by the word 'Russell'; or This experience *may* not have been preceded by the word 'Russell'; 'possible' and 'may' are being used in an entirely different sense.[2]

Although Moore does not use the term 'equivocation' to characterize Russell's mistake, he is, in effect, as I have pointed out elsewhere,[3] accusing skeptics, including Russell, of having committed the *fallacy of equivocation*. Moore's point can be made quite simply. Even though it is *possible for* my computer to be in the kitchen, it is not *possible that* it is. I am currently using it to write this chapter on Moore, and I am doing so in my study. What Moore is arguing is that although it is factually true that human beings do dream, do hallucinate, are subject to perceptual errors of various sorts, including illusions, these facts do not in any way show that one might on any given occasion be dreaming, hallucinating, experiencing an illusion, etc. Although I have dreamt that I was in my study doing a variety of things, this fact does not in any way imply the possibility that I am now dreaming—that there is even the slightest bit of concrete evidence that I am. According to Moore, the onus is on the skeptic to establish that it is always possible that any human being is at anytime dreaming, hallucinating, etc.—that there is always empirical evidence that any given human being is currently dreaming, hallucinating, etc. But, says Moore, no skeptic has ever succeeded in establishing this possibility. At best they have only succeeded in showing that it is always possible for any human to dream, hallucinate, etc. Moore's argument is compelling, but as I said previously, it is not airtight. Elsewhere, I have argued against Moore by arguing that "possible that p" is not always an *inappropriate* description of those cases where there is *no* concrete evidence that p. Let us imagine that two women have pulled into a parking space in front of their local bank with the intention of

44

withdrawing money. As they get out of the car to go into the bank someone runs out of the bank with a bag of money in one hand and a revolver in the other. A bank guard in pursuit of the robber yells, "Stop him, he just robbed the bank." The women register both shock and recognition regarding the robber. One of them asks the robber, "John what in the world is going on?" He shoves her aside, and jumps into a car driven by an accomplice. They speed away. When the women are interrogated, and shown what the bank's cameras have recorded, they break down and confess that the robber is the son of one of them, and the husband of the other. The police apprehend the suspect at home. When confronted with the evidence against him, he protests his innocence, although he has no alibi. He was at home alone all day and was not seen by anyone. His prospects are slim appear to be quite slim. They start to improve, however, when Sherlock Holmes appears at the police station and claims, as he characteristically does, that the police are mistaken. He claims that it may not have been John who robbed the bank. "Do you have any concrete evidence that he did not rob the bank, was he seen somewhere else at the time the bank was robbed, was he at work?" asks Inspector Lestrade. Holmes replies that he does not have any evidence to disprove John robbed the bank, but that there are facts which must not be discounted. Years ago, when he was pursuing his arch enemy Professor Moriarty through the streets of London, Moriaty escaped near St James Hospital. The next day Holmes read in the *Times* that someone had kidnapped a male child from that very same hospital, and that this child was a member of a set of identical male twins. The child was never recovered. Holmes reminds Inspector Lestrade that Moriarty has always boasted that he will commit the perfect crime. Holmes then argues that if Moriaty was responsible for the kidnapping, the scenario of this crime is consistent with the hypothesis that it was Moriarity's attempt to commit the perfect crime. Moriarity could have raised the boy to be a criminal, kept close watch on John and his family, knew that the women of the house always did their banking on Tuesdays, and knew that John never left the house on that day. On the basis of these considerations, Holmes concludes that it is possible *that* John did not commit the robbery.

In short, my case reveals that "possible that not p" does not require there to be concrete evidence that p is not the case. Instead, all that is required is that one provide *good reasons* or be able to provide a plausible case that not p. Like Holmes, the skeptic offers a "fact-based scenario" which would, in spite of any concrete evidence favoring p, establish that not p remains a factual possibility. This is precisely what the skeptic does when he points out that as a matter of fact humans do hallucinate and dream, and are often deceived by their senses.[4]

Moore treats the skeptical argument based upon the possibility of the existence of a malevolent deity differently from the dream, hallucination, and perceptual errors arguments. He does not attempt to refute it by labeling it an "equivocation." The claim that it is possible for humans to dream, hallucinate etc. is an empirical possibility. The argument based upon the existence of the evil demon is not based upon an empirical or factual possibility. According to Moore:

> It is, I think, an argument which introduces quite new considerations, of which I have said nothing so far, and which lead us to the root of the difference between Russell and me. I take it that Russell is here asserting that it is *logically possible* that this particular percept of mine [There was a *sound* like "Russell" a little while ago] ...was in fact produced in me by a malicious demon ... and that, therefore, I cannot know for certain what I think I know...The questions we have to consider are, then, simply these three: What is meant by saying that it is *logically possible* that this percept was produced by a malicious demon? Is it true that this is logically possible? And: If it is true, does it follow that I don't know for certain that it was *not* produced by a malicious demon?[5]

Moore proceeds to answer the first of these questions by arguing that what Russell must have meant is that "The proposition 'this percept was produced by an evil demon' is *not* logically incompatible with anything you know *immediately*." [6] Moore concedes that if this is what Russell meant, then what Russell meant to say is true, and thus that the only remaining question to be answered is the third question. Although Moore agrees with Russell that his knowledge that the object he has in his hand is a pencil does not follow logically from anything he does know immediately [various sense-data], he, nevertheless, disagrees with Russell's conclusion because he thinks he does know with certainty, not only that he has a pencil in his hand, but also many other propositions of this variety. He claims that Russell's reasons for thinking otherwise are: (a) that one's belief that he does know for certain, for example, that he has a pencil in his hand, since it is not based on anything known immediately, must be based upon an "analogical" or "inductive" argument; and (b) that any belief based upon such an argument cannot qualify as certain knowledge. Moore agrees with Russell that (a) is true, but disagrees with (b). He claims that analogical or inductive arguments can yield certain knowledge. And, moreover, that in order to be convinced that Russell's argument is correct, and thus that he cannot know that he has a pencil in his hand, he must accept four distinct assumptions or premises, namely: (1) that he does not know immediately that he has a pencil in his hand; (2) that it does not follow immediately from anything he does know immediately; (3) if (1) and (2) are true, his belief that he has a pencil in his hand must be based upon an analogical or inductive argument; and finally (4) that what is based upon such arguments cannot qualify as certain knowledge. Moore then claims that he is more certain that he has a pencil in his hand than he is certain that *any* one of these four assumptions is true, "let alone *all* four." "Nay more: I do not think that it is *rational* to be as certain of any one of these four propositions, as of the proposition that I know that this is a pencil." He hedges his bet, however, by asking "how on earth is it to be decided which of these two things it is rational to be most certain of?" and by leaving this question unanswered.[7] I think we can do better than this.

I think we *can* establish that it is more rational for one to sometimes be certain that he has a pencil in his hand, than to be convinced by any of Russell's arguments for skepticism, including the one based upon the possibility that a malevolent deity exists. I will address this issue further in the chapter on the topic of certainty when I take up the question regarding the differences between Moore and Wittgenstein regarding that topic.

---

[1] All four of which are in Moore's *Philosophical Papers* (1959).

[2] Moore (1959) p. 219.

[3] Merrill and Odell (1983) pp. 62-64.

[4] Odell (2000) p. 59.

[5] Moore (1959) p. 223.

[6] Ibid., p. 225.

[7] Ibid., pp. 224-226.

6

Defending Common Sense, and Proving that an External World Exists

It is one thing to show that the arguments in favor of classical philosophical skepticism fail to substantiate it. It is another thing to provide a defense in favor of the common sense view that we do quite often know with certainty that physical objects, other persons, our own selves, etc. do exist, and have existed in the past, and do have and have had certain specifiable properties, and do stand and have stood in certain specifiable relations to other objects. Moore attempted to accomplish both tasks. In the last chapter I examined his challenge to skepticism. In this chapter I will be looking carefully at his defense of common sense. I will also be looking at his attempt to prove that an external world exists. These two topics are intimately related. His proof that there is an external world is founded upon common sense.

With the possible exception of the nineteenth century Scottish philosopher Thomas Reid, no philosopher's fame rests more securely on defending common sense than does Moore's. Most philosophers are not only dismissive regarding its validity; they are largely contemptuous of it. This was particularly true of most philosophers when Moore entered into the fray. At that time English philosophy was dominated by the Hegelians, and they were firmly entrenched at

Cambridge. It took great courage on Moore's part to attack such highly esteemed Cambridge Hegelians as J. Ellis McTaggart, and F.H. Bradley. Moore is often identified with the child in the fable "The Emperor's New Clothes." Like the child of the fable, Moore refuses to be swayed by the gullibility of those who sought the approval of the Emperor. But unlike the child of the fable, Moore knew precisely what he was doing, and he appreciated the risks involved.

Nowhere does Moore state the case for common sense in more detail than in his 1925 article, "A Defense of Common Sense." Moore begins this essay by stating a large number of propositions that he claims to know with certainty to be true, even though he admits that he is uncertain regarding their correct analysis.[1] His list is long but we need not consider it in its entirety because all of them can be reduced to just four kinds of proposition—the same four linked to the four forms of skepticism Moore attributed to Russell in his essay on skepticism. They are propositions about: the past; physical objects; other persons; and the self.

Moore views the typical philosopher's claim—that we do not know with certainty any of these propositions--with suspicion rather than respect. He reminds us that our ordinary or common sense concepts of "knowing" and "certainty" *legitimize* his claim to know propositions of all four of the kinds under consideration. These concepts enable us to distinguish between knowing, for example, that something is a hand, and being uncertain that it is—the later being the appropriate description for the kind of case I instantiated as a case of forensic anthropology, p. 28 above. The skeptic's rejection of the conceptual framework of common sense would, if it were accepted, eliminate this important distinction. There would no longer exist a use for it.

Many philosophers, even non-skeptics, however, immediately rejected the point of view he expressed in the article under consideration. They argued that although they would agree with Moore that we do quite often claim to know with certainty various propositions of the four kinds under scrutiny, we are, nonetheless, *not* justified in doing so. They claimed that it is one thing to remind us of this fact about ordinary usage; it is another thing to show that it has philosophical significance. In short, what these critics argued is that Moore's philosophical position on this issue is just highly reiterative question begging.

Other philosophers, including Norman Malcolm, and more recently, Avrum Stroll, defend Moore against this charge. Malcolm claims that although "Moore never gave a satisfactory account of what he was doing," that "Moore himself was confused about what he was doing,"[2] one can defend him by utilizing an often quoted passage from Wittgenstein's *Investigations*, "Philosophy may in no way interfere with the actual use of language: it can in the end only describe it." According to Malcolm, "in order to grasp" Wittgenstein's point, "one must understand what is right in Moore's defense of ordinary language."[3]

Malcolm's interpretation of what Moore is doing is that he is offering a meta-argument against any argument that concludes that we do not know with certainty any propositions of the four kinds under consideration. Malcolm's interpretation of Moore's argument can be put thus:

(P1) If there is a correct use for sentences like 'It is known for certain that both my wife and I set sail for Europe yesterday,' then any argument that is alleged to show that no sentence of this kind can have a legitimate use is, if not invalid, certainly unsound.

(P2) There are correct uses for sentences like the one stated above. Imagine my having said it in response to another person's claim that my wife and I were elsewhere, when I know that a large number of people saw us at the pier.

(C) Any argument that is or could be alleged to show that there is no legitimate use for the sentence in question, is, if not invalid, most certainly unsound.

Although I think that Malcolm is on the right track regarding Moore's position, I think that Malcolm's way of putting it is unfortunate. I am not convinced that *every* philosopher who claims to be a skeptic regarding the four kinds of proposition under consideration would want to deny that there is a correct or proper use for sentences like 'It is known for certain that both my wife and I set sail for Europe yesterday.' To deny as the skeptic does that such claims as are made by using this sentence are justified, is not to say that they do not have a legitimate use. The skeptic could argue that such claims as the one in question are *conventionally*, but not *epistemologically* justified. Malcolm could admit this, however, and argue that they are just confused and do not realize that their position entails the view that there is no correct use for S—that is Wittgenstein's position.

There is another problem with Malcolm's presentation of Moore's position. It can be argued that in order to justify the charge that one is misusing a sentence one would have to be able to say what a correct use of it would be. Can anyone do this regarding any sentence? Not according to Gilbert Ryle, who claims, "we can ask whether a person knows how to use...a certain word. But we cannot ask whether he knows how to use a certain sentence."[4]

This objection, which is not itself immune to criticism, need not deter us, however. We can offset this difficulty with Malcolm's interpretation of Moore by replacing "correct or proper use of a sentence like 'It is known for certain that my wife and I set sail for Europe yesterday,' with "correct or proper use of the phrase 'known for certain that' in claims where 'known for certain that' modifies some empirical state of affairs. More importantly, however, there is another way of interpreting Moore's defense of common sense that not only answers the skeptic's charge that it is irrelevant, but also challenges Malcolm's interpretation of Moore because it puts Moore at odds with Wittgenstein's remark concerning the exemption proof status of "actual language."

One could interpret what Moore was doing in the essay in defense of common sense as not only providing an explication and defense of the common sense view of the world, but also as providing a clarification of how it differs from what philosophers have been trying to do, which is to provide an analysis of what we *actually* know when we know with certainty such things as: this is a hand I am holding out in front of me. Moore does, in fact from the outset, as we have seen; concede that he does not know what the right analysis of the claims of common sense would be. On this interpretation, which Arthur Murphy has explicated in his essay for the Schilpp volume on Moore's philosophy "Moore's Defense of Common Sense," what Moore has shown is:

> ...that it is quite possible to understand statements about observed material objects and other selves, in their ordinary or popular meaning, and to know their truth for certain, without knowing what their correct analysis is or which among competing epistemologies gives the right account of what it is that we are "ultimately" knowing when we know them...This brings the whole issue between common sense and epistemology to a new focus...The essential point...is not that the plain man has some primitive but infallible way of knowing the answer to the

problems which excite epistemologists, but that he requires no such knowledge in order to justify his claim to "know" in a quite clear and proper sense, the existence and observable nature of objects and persons in his environment.[5]

Given this interpretation of Moore, we would expect Murphy to claim that Moore and his critics are both right because "their dispute is not about any matter of fact." It is only a dispute regarding which language is to be preferred over the other, or to put the matter in terms of the distinction I introduced a few paragraphs ago, it is only a dispute regarding whether the conventional or the epistemological account is preferable. Is the language of the common sense, which talks of certainty concerning material things, to be preferred over the language of the epistemologist, which would restrict talk of certain knowledge to talk about the ultimate givens of perception (sense-data), or is the reverse preferable? And the correct answer to this question might well turn out to be dependent upon context, whether it is an epistemological or an everyday context. But, Murphy does not let the matter rest here. This interpretation of Moore is far too egalitarian for Murphy's tastes. Instead, he argues that although this way of interpreting Moore involves "a measure of truth," it is, nevertheless "more misleading than helpful." He thinks the right way to read Moore is to read him to be saying: (1) that there is no "better or more ultimate way of knowing the facts about the world" than that of common sense; and (2) that the ultimate objects of perceptual knowledge are sense-data is not something which analysis reveals as the ultimate objects of knowledge, but rather is something which analysis "imposes upon the perceptual situation."[6] And Murphy also thinks that the question as to whether or not this is Moore's actual view is not as important as the idea it suggests, namely, that:

> Propositions about perceived material objects need have no more "ultimate" subjects than their ostensible subjects, the material objects perceptually indicated and observed. And the known truth of such propositions need not wait upon any epistemological analysis of sense-data, for it was not about the results of such analysis that the propositions were asserted. Any such result, moreover, if it is a correct analysis, must be compatible with the fact that such propositions as "this is my hand" are known to be true.[7]

This is an interesting way of regarding Moore's defense of common sense, and one to which I will return briefly in the next chapter. For now, let me turn to Stroll's defense of Moore.

Like Malcolm, Stroll raises doubts concerning how fully Moore realized just what he was doing. He thinks Moore failed to recognize the difference between *personal* (or psychological certainty) and *objective* (or epistemological) certainty—one might *feel* certain that he is the tallest person in the world when as a matter of fact there exist many people taller than he is. Stroll also thinks that Moore failed to realize that there are two distinctly different kinds of proposition of the four sorts under consideration. There are those of the sort exemplified by "There is on my desk a cup of coffee," and there are those like "There are human beings and they all have to die." Both kinds can be said to be known with certainty to be true. Both kinds are contingent—their denials are not contradictions. But the latter, unlike the former are "not known to be true only in certain circumstances." Stoll refers to this characteristic feature of the latter kind of proposition as "context independence."[8] Stroll claims that a proposition must be context independent to be a constituent of the common sense view. And he recognizes, and lists, other characteristics besides context dependence, which propositions must possess in order to qualify as constituents of a *defensible* version common sense view.[9] This defensible, or well worked out, formulation of the common sense view he refers to as a "form of foundationalism," and attributes it to Wittgenstein. He credits Moore with having started the ball rolling in the right direction, but credits Wittgenstein with having found the precise projection for the ball's path. Stroll refers to those propositions which constitute the common sense view as "primordial propositions," and refers to the "knowledge they express," as "primordial knowledge," and claims that:

> An indefinitely long list of such propositions embodies a kind of pre-technical knowledge that, I take it, is what Moore means by the common sense view of the world. With certain important qualifications, we can also say that some such conception is what Wittgenstein has in mind when he says that there is something that "stands fast for all of us."[10]

I will return to this view of Stroll's in the next chapter. I want now to turn to Moore's "Proof of an External World," which appeared originally in 1939.

According to Moore, his proof of an external world is meant to meet the challenge of those philosophers who claim that although the external world might well exist, no one could ever prove that it does, and that the existence of external objects must be accepted on *faith*. According to Moore, these philosophers are mistaken because, he can assert to know with certainty, as he holds up both of his hands, that "Here is one hand, and here is another." By parity of reason, if someone tells me that he has a sixth toe on his right foot, and I express disbelief, he can, in the ordinary sense of the word 'prove,' *prove* to me that he does have a sixth toe by removing his right shoe and right sock and displaying his extra appendage. According to Moore, any proof must satisfy three conditions if it is to qualify as such. First, its premise or premises must be different from the conclusion. Second, its advocate must know with certainty that its premise or premises are true. And finally, the conclusion must follow from the premise or premises. Moore claims that his proof meets all three conditions, and that one could, by following his example, provide "thousands of different" proofs that there are things outside or external to us, and thus that there is an external world. He also "proves" by similar means that objects outside us existed in the past. He recognizes, however, that his proofs will not satisfy all philosophers; many will "still feel that I have not given any satisfactory proof of the point in question."[11]

Moore attempts to explain the hesitation that other philosophers feel about his "proof" to be based in part upon the fact that these philosophers would not accept his proof unless he also proved to their satisfaction that his premises were true. But, according to Moore, what they really want is not a proof of his premises; instead they want "something like a general statement as to how *any* propositions of this sort may be proved." Such a demand cannot, however, concedes Moore, be given, and what is more "if this is what is meant by proof of the existence of external things, I do not believe that any proof of the existence of external things can be given." The reason one cannot prove that his premises are true, as Moore views the matter, is that one cannot prove that one is not dreaming. He claims to have conclusive evidence that he is not now dreaming, but concedes that "that is a very different thing from being able to prove it." In this essay he does not proceed as he did in "Four Forms of Scepticism." Here he does not rely on the distinction between "possible that" and "possible for," even though the two essays in question were written not more than a year apart. But he does argue that the mere fact that he cannot prove that he is not dreaming, and thus that he does not have a proof of his premises, does not mean that he must accept his premises "merely as a matter of faith." Instead he holds, "I can know things, which I cannot prove: and among the things which I certainly did know...were the premises of my two proofs."[12] What Moore is saying is, although he may not himself be fully aware that that is what he is saying, can be put in the following way—the absence of a criterion in terms of necessary and sufficient conditions, an essential condition, is not, as the skeptic would have it, a valid reason for claiming that one can never know that one is not dreaming. All that is required is that ordinary criteria—those we rely on everyday—be satisfied. To borrow an example from Wittgenstein, an example I have utilized previously, the skeptic's position amounts to the same thing as alleging that one cannot say with certainty that chess is a game because we cannot specify an essential condition for being a game. Alice Ambrose, in her essay for the Schilpp volume, "Moore's 'Proof' of an External world," casts Moore's views in Wittgensteinian mold, without realizing, or perhaps only choosing not to disclose, that that is what she is doing when she says:

> He has not himself shown the pointlessness of the sceptic's attempted revisions of language, for he has not seen clearly what the sceptic is doing and consequently has not shown what he is doing. But in calling attention to ordinary language...he takes us the first step toward seeing what the sceptic is doing and that what he is doing is pointless. For reminding one of how language is ordinarily used is a way of making one feel there is something absurd about what the sceptic propounds.[13]

What Ambrose is doing, even if she is not aware of it, when she credits him with having called attention *unknowingly* to the unhappy consequences inherent in ignoring ordinary language, is attributing to Moore a precursor to the view expressed by Wittgenstein in paragraph 109 of the *Investigations* when he says about philosophical problems:

> These are, of course, not empirical problems; they are solved, rather, by looking into the workings of our language...The problems are solved, not by giving new information, but by arranging what we have always known. Philosophy is the bewitchment of our intelligence by means of language.[14]

It must have occurred to the reader by now that although this book traverses routes originally charted by Moore, it inevitably invites, even coerces, the reader to travel the same routes by following Moore's charts as refined and modified by Wittgenstein. The reason for this is twofold. First, our interest in the issues Moore raises need not, in fact should not, and for the philosophically inclined cannot, end with just a rehash of what Moore has said about them. What is even more important are those advances have been stimulated by Moore's efforts. Second, a full appreciation of Moore's immense contribution to philosophy is not possible without appreciation of the consequences of his work on Wittgenstein. One of the most revealing topics on which to concentrate in order to enhance our appreciation of Moore's effects upon Wittgenstein is the topic of certainty—the topic of the next chapter.

---

[1] Moore (1925) p.33.
[2] Malcolm (1963) p. 177.
[3] Malcolm (1963) pp. 181-183.
[4] Ryle (1963) pp. 119-120.
[5] Schilpp (1952) pp. 310-311.
[6] Ibid., pp. 311-313.
[7] Ibid., p. 317.
[8] Stroll (1994) pp. 32-39.
[9] Ibid., pp.149-159.
[10] Ibid., p.39.
[11] Moore (1959) pp. 145-148.
[12] Ibid., pp. 148-150.
[13] Schilpp (1952) pp. 415-417.
[14] Wittgenstein (1958) p. 47^e.

7

On Certainty
and Wittgenstein's Response

We have already seen how Moore attempts to defend our commonsense notion of certainty. It is time now to contrast his views with those of Wittgenstein, whom he greatly influenced, so much so that Wittgenstein's last burst of philosophical creativity was motivated by his preoccupation with Moore's claims about the nature of certainty. Moore devoted a great deal of time and effort to understand and analyze the concept of "certainty." His most extended foray in this direction is a paper entitled "On Certainty." Wittgenstein's work on this subject is also entitled *On Certainty*, which is, according to its editors, G.E.M. Anscombe and G. H. von Wright, a book length presentation of "first-draft material," which Wittgenstein "did not live to excerpt and polish."[1] As we have already seen, Moore also expressed views on this subject in "Proof of the External World," "A Defense of Common Sense," and "Four Forms of Scepticism."

In the paper on common sense, Moore lists, as I pointed out previously, a number of propositions that he knows with certainty to be true. In the skepticism paper, he claims that there are four kinds of things about which he is certain regarding their existence: physical objects, other persons, the past, and his own self. In the last chapter I claimed that his lists from the common sense paper could all be reduced to the four forms of proposition he enumerates in the skepticism paper. He begins "On Certainty" by making seven assertions that he claims to know with certainty to be true, each of which can also be reduced to one of the four forms of propositions featured in the skepticism paper. In addition, Moore claims that many philosophers would deny that anyone could be certain about any of these propositions.

In all of these essays, the propositions about which he is certain are propositions the denials of which are non-contradictions. Their denials can be true. The first one of the seven assertions he makes at the outset of "On Certainty" is "I am present, as you all can see, in a room and not in the open air." Clearly, its denial, like the denials of each of the other six, is not self-contradictory. It is *possible for* Moore to have been elsewhere. Because their denials are not self-contradictories, they are, according to Moore, what logicians and philosophers refer to as *contingent propositions*.

Moore insists, in opposition to the skeptics, that the mere fact that a proposition is contingent does not entail that it cannot be known to be true.[2] Moreover, according to Moore, the fact that his seven assertions are contingent does not entail that when he made them he did not know them to be true. He says, "From the fact that they are contingent it does not follow, in the case of any single one among them, that it was *possible that* the proposition in question was false."[3] The upshot of these initial considerations is the same as that previously noted in Chapter IV, where I mostly focused the discussion on "Four Forms of Scepticism," namely, that although it is *possible for* any one of these seven assertions to be false, it is not *possible that* any one of them actually is false.

Moore's next move is to argue that the fact that the seven propositions in question are contingent is "quite compatible with its being true that every one of those seven things that I asserted was not only true but *absolutely certain*." Which is to say, according to Moore that "if any person whatever, does at a given time know that a given proposition p is true, then it follows that that person could say with truth at that time 'It is absolutely certain that p'."[4] In order to establish this point he digresses to meet the kind of objection which insists that there is an important difference in meaning between 'It is certain that p' (where p is any one of the seven assertions that Moore has asserted) and the following three: 'I am certain that p,' 'I feel certain that p,' and 'I know for certain that p.' That alleged difference is, according to Moore, that anyone asserting (1)-(3) would be making assertions "different from and logically independent of what another person would be saying who made the same three assertions," because the referent of the word 'I' would be different for each speaker. Moore concedes that "from the fact that I feel certain of or know for certain a given thing it *never* follows, in the case of any other person whatever, that he feels certain of or knows the thing in question, nor from the fact that he does does it ever follow that I do." He also acknowledges that the assertion that it is certain that there are windows in that wall, *appears* to convey a meaning "not relative to the person who says it." We must not, however, according to Moore, be led astray by what appears to be the case regarding the meaning of 'It is certain that p.' Moore argues that "in spite of appearances, the meaning of 'It is certain that p' is relative to the person who says it," because, according to Moore, "if anybody asserts 'It is certain that p' part of what he is asserting is that he himself knows that p is true."[5]

He continues by arguing that, in addition to being contingent, each one of the seven propositions that he asserted at the beginning of his paper shares the characteristic of implying that *an external world* exists. A third characteristic common to all seven is, according to Moore, that they are "at least partly *based* on 'the then present evidence of' my senses'." A fourth and final characteristic common to all is, according to Moore, that "if *they* were not certain, then no proposition which implies the existence of anything external to the mind of the person who makes it is ever certain."[6] He alleges that all seven are certain, but acknowledges, as we have seen him do in "Proof of the External World," that many philosophers have argued that no proposition that implies the existence of anything external to the mind can ever be certain. He then proceeds to discuss "one of the types of argument which have sometimes been alleged to show that nobody ever has known for certain anything about a world external to his mind."

The argument he chooses to discuss is the dream argument. In his paper on skepticism he argued, as we have seen, that although the skeptic is justified in claiming that it is always *possible for* one to dream, it is not the case that it is always *possible that* one is dreaming. Although he has, as I pointed out a few paragraphs ago, used this distinction in the paper under consideration to characterize what is meant by the predicate 'is contingent,' he does not utilize it here to refute the dream argument. Instead, he produces an argument that is at best exasperatingly inconclusive and at worst simply wrongheaded.

He argues that the dream argument turns on the truth of the "premise" that "Some at least of the sensory experiences which you are having now are similar in important respects to dream-images which have actually occurred in dreams," and although he has qualms about its suitability as a premise in the skeptic's argument, he concedes that it is true. His qualm is a serious one, namely, that anyone who uses this premise, and also asserts that no one can ever be certain that he is not dreaming, is guilty of an inconsistency. I will return to this qualm of his after I have discussed his argument against the dream argument. He admits that "it is logically possible that all the sensory experiences I am having now should be mere dream-images," and concludes that if the *sensory* experiences he was then having were all the experiences he was then having, he would have to admit that he does not know for certain that he is not dreaming. But since the present sensory experiences are not the only ones he is having, he is also having memories of the immediate past, these experiences taken together "*may be*," he claims "sufficient to enable me to know that I am not dreaming." Then he adds, that *even* if it is not sufficient, this conjunction of experiences provides as good a reason for *affirming* that he does know that he is not dreaming, as are any of the skeptic's reasons for *denying* that he does know that he is not dreaming.[7] But he also makes a stronger claim:

> It is certainly logically possible that I *should have* been dreaming now; I *might* have been dreaming now; and therefore the proposition that I *am* dreaming now is not self-contradictory. But what I am in doubt of is whether it is logically possible that I should *both* be having all the sensory experience and the memories that I have and yet be dreaming. The conjunction of the proposition that I have these sense experiences and memories with the proposition that I am dreaming does seem to me to be very likely self-contradictory.[8]

This is Moore at his worst.[9] In the first place, I do not see why he doesn't accuse the defender of the dream argument of committing the fallacy of "equivocation" as he did in "Four Forms of Scepticism," which was written around the same time as the work under consideration. Since I defended the skeptic against Moore's accusation that he is equivocating on the word 'possible' in Chapter V, the reader may wonder why I bring it up here? I do so because I think that in spite of its faults, it is a much better argument than the argument he advances in passages under consideration.

The major problem with Moore's argument against scepticism in "On Certainty" concerns the additional force that memory impressions are supposed to have. I do not recognize a sufficiently significant enough difference between memory impressions and presently existing sensory impressions to convince me that the former adds enough force to convince the skeptic. Memory impressions are always, to borrow from Hume, less vivid and lively than presently occurring sensory impressions. I am almost always far less sure of my memory impressions, for example, that I had an apple yesterday, than I am, for example, of such facts as the fact that I am now eating an apple. Adding to the evidence that I am not presently dreaming by acquiring further presently existing sensory data, pinching myself, striking the objects "seen," etc. would be far more likely to convince me that I am not dreaming than would any recollections I might have about the past.

But what about Moore's parting shot, his claim that the conjunction of these two kinds of impression with the proposition that he is dreaming is "very likely self-contradictory." In the first place, whether or not any given proposition is self-contradictory seems to me to be easily decided, and not a matter warranting any indecision. All that is required to settle such matters is to examine the denial of the proposition in question to determine whether or not it is a contradiction. Be that as it may, however, I do not see how the addition of the memory impressions to presently existing sensory impressions adds *any* credence whatever to the claim that my present momentary sense impressions are inconsistent with the claim that I might now be dreaming. Perhaps, my present momentary sensory experiences are inconsistent with the fact that I might now be dreaming, but adding my present memories of the recent past does not settle the matter one way or the other.

Previously, I promised to return to the qualm that Moore expressed regarding the skeptic's premise, "Some at least of the sensory experiences which you are having now are similar in important respects to dream-images which have actually occurred in dreams." Moore's qualm is that anyone who uses this premise, and who also asserts that no one can ever be certain that he is not dreaming, is guilty of an inconsistency. He defends this idea by arguing that anyone who uses this premise implies that he "knows it to be true," which implies "that he himself knows that dreams have occurred." Moore asks:

Can anybody possibly know that dreams have occurred, if, at the time, he does not himself know that he is not dreaming? If he *is* dreaming, it may be that he is only dreaming that dreams have occurred; and if he does not know that he is not dreaming, can he possibly know that he is *not* only dreaming that dreams have occurred? Can he possibly know therefore that dreams *have* occurred? I do not think that he can; and therefore I think that

61

anyone who uses this premiss and also asserts the conclusion that nobody ever knows that he is not dreaming, is guilty of an inconsistency. By using this premiss he implies that he himself knows that dreams have occurred; while, if this conclusion is true, it follows that he himself does not know that he is not dreaming, and therefore does not know that he is not only dreaming that dreams have occurred.[10]

This is probably Moore's best argument against the skeptic's use of the dream argument, which only goes to prove that there is more than just a grain of truth to Wittgenstein's often quoted remark that he did not think that Moore would recognize a solution to a philosophical problem if you gave him one. This argument, which I shall refer to as "the dream paradox," may well be valid. Elsewhere,[11] I have argued that even if I am right, and Moore is wrong, in thinking that the skeptic's principle argument in favor of his position is an *equivocation* fallacy, an independent argument can, nevertheless, be constructed to show that philosophical skepticism must be mistaken. And it seems to me that my argument incorporates the same basic insight that underlies Moore's "dream paradox." According to classical philosophical skeptics, we can never be certain of the truth of any of our beliefs other than those whose denials are contradictions (tautologies) and those which describe only a object presently existing in a sensory field (beliefs about sense-data). This way of stating the skeptic's position involves the use of the *exclusive* formulation that I introduced above.[12] Skeptics frequently discuss and utilize the dream argument, as well as other arguments, to exclude from the realm of certain knowledge: beliefs about Gods, physical objects, other persons, the self, the past and the future. There is, however, one class of beliefs that the exclusive formulation excludes, and which the skeptic has, to my knowledge, never even considered. The following is an example of that kind of belief:

> The word 'dog' means "A domesticated carnivorous mammal raised in a wide variety of breeds and probably originally derived from several wild species."

It is a definition. Definitions are not analytical—their denials are not contradictions. Nor do they describe sense-data. Since they are neither of these kinds of belief, we must, if we accept the skeptic's account of this matter, as formulated in the exclusive mode, assign them to the realm of the doubtful. But if they are so regarded, how can anyone be certain about anything that he claims? All claims are, of necessity, expressed in language, and language use presupposes the truth of indefinitely many definitions. Since all of the skeptic's arguments consist in various claims, it follows that all of his arguments are themselves doubtful. Why then, should anyone take them seriously? Is this not the same question that Moore's dream paradox poses for the skeptic? But even if I am mistaken in my supposition that Moore and I share is the same insight, it is clear that my insight is precisely parallel to the insight that motivated Wittgenstein to respond to the skeptic's concern regarding such questions as "How do you know that this is a dog?" with the philosophically perplexing answer, "I know English!"

Wittgenstein's interest in the skeptical issue was motivated in large part by Moore's efforts to refute it. Throughout his work *On Certainty* Wittgenstein refers to Moore, and at one place compares Moore's work on certainty to a "painted stage-set" in so far as one recognizes what it is supposed to represent from "a long way off," but when perceived from up close it is nothing but "a lot of patches of different colors, which are all highly ambiguous and do not provide any certainty whatever."[13]   In general, Moore and Wittgenstein share a similar outlook regarding the *acceptability* of skepticism, yet they differ regarding its *viability*.   Avrum Stroll in his book on both philosophers argues that:

> Moore presupposes that the sceptic's doubts make sense and can be answered by asserting that he Moore knows this or that p with certainty. But Wittgenstein's understanding is deeper. He shows that what the sceptic wishes to say cannot be said without violating the constraints that would make the question sensible. No such answer as Moore wishes to provide is thus possible or needed. Scepticism is not merely mistaken, as Moore thinks; it is, as Wittgenstein demonstrates, conceptually aberrant.[14]

I agree with Stroll, but I want to insist that had Moore fully understood the implications of what I have referred to as his "dream paradox," he also might well have recognized that skepticism is incoherent or "conceptually aberrant."

From the perspective of many other philosophers, Wittgenstein's position on the certainty issue is revolutionary—yet it   is a position with which all of us are familiar. This familiarity is not, however, of the *cognitive* variety, and that is why Wittgenstein's views on this

63

subject surprise us. It is a familiar way of *acting*, but it has to be revealed to us at the cognitive level in order for us to appreciate it. And, this is what Wittgenstein attempts to do for us. He painstakingly explicates the underlying principles that govern our linguistic practices regarding that interrelated set of concepts relevant to the topic of scepticism: doubting, knowing, believing, judging, learning, being certain, and feeling certain—concepts that are systematically misapprehended and misappropriated by both skeptical and non–skeptical philosophers.

Doubting, when it is properly understood, turns out to be just one human practice or language game among others. Like chess, it is mastered by engaging in it. Over time one becomes a master of the game—to the extent that one can play it without violating its rules. This is not to deny that there are levels of expertise. Grand masters play the game at a higher level than do most practitioners of the game, but this is a difference in *strategy*, and not in mastery of fundamentals.

Doubting takes place within the *confines* of the community. Children are not born doubting, they are trained to do so. They have to master it just as they have to master any other activity. They are not born walking, or talking, as they are born feeling, and crying. Being certain, unlike feeling certain, is acting in specifiable ways. One can, in fact, according Wittgenstein, be certain even when one does not feel certain. When, for example, I ride a horse, something which I have done most of my life, I am rarely aware of my legs engaging with his girth, my hands making very slight adjustments on the reins, or my seat being adjusted to control his pace, yet I can, by concentrating on any of these things, feel them happening. Awareness that these actions are taking place is *not* necessary for a successful equestrian outing, but their occurrence *is* necessary for such an outing to take place. A successful ride depends on the occurrence of these discrete actions on my part, the result of both training and practice, and in this way they are like what Wittgenstein refers to as *hinge* propositions. About them he says:

> That is to say, the *questions* that we raise and our *doubts* depend on the fact that some propositions are exempt from doubt, are as it were like hinges on which those turn.[15]

Wittgenstein uses the concept of "hinge propositions" to make his case against skepticism, which he summarizes by saying that the "game of doubting itself presupposes certainty."[16] Avrum Stroll

64

provides a praiseworthy exposition of Wittgenstein's views on certainty in his *Moore and Wittgenstein on Certainty*. Yet Stroll does not seem to realize that although Wittgenstein never mentions hinge propositions in the *Investigations*, his discussion of both the "standard metre" and the "sepia color sample" in the *Investigations* are, in spite of the fact that they are used there to make a different point, importantly relevant to the topic of "certainty." They are extremely useful for understanding what hinge propositions are. The relevant remarks from the *Investigations* are:

> There is *one* thing of which one can say neither that it is one metre long, nor that it is not one metre long, and that is the standard metre in Paris.—But this is, of course, not to ascribe any extraordinary property to it, but only to mark its peculiar role in the language-game, of measuring with a metre-rule.—Let us imagine samples of colour being preserved in Paris like the standard metre. We define "sepia" means the colour of the standard sepia which is there kept hermetically sealed. Then it will make no sense to say of this sample either that it is of this colour or that it is not... This sample is an instrument of the language used in ascriptions of colour. In this language-game it is not something that is represented, but is a means of representation.[17]

Any claim like "This is my left hand," said when, as Moore does, one is holding up one's left hand, can be said to a paradigm of one's language. They are instruments of the language-game. Doubts about one's own hands, for example that they are as beautiful, or as hairy as they used to be, depend upon, or are hinged upon, the certainty that they are one's own hands. The overall or general language-game, English, depends upon the existence of innumerable and miniscule language-games, or rules, or *definitions*, without which we could not speak or think cognitively. No challenge or doctrine of any sort, including skepticism, could exist unless it is hinged in those definitions that comprise the language in which it is couched.

But this is not to say that hinge propositions of the sort explicated via the "standard metre case" are never doubtful. Although, as previously noted, Wittgenstein does not make explicit use of the "standard metre" or "sepia" cases in *On Certainty*, he does, I think, make *implicit* reference to such cases when he says in section 98, "...the same proposition may get treated at one time as something to test by experience at another as a rule of testing."[18] If the standard metre in Paris were replaced by a different and more precise standard of measurement, one could imagine that someone in possession of the old measuring rule might take it to Paris to determine if it is really a metre long. The point I want to make on the basis of Wittgenstein's remark is that any example of the kind of hinge proposition that would serve to ostensively define a word could itself be challenged under certain kinds of extenuating circumstances.

Definitions like 'democracy' means "government by the people exercised either directly or through elected representatives," and the one I previously provided for the word 'dog' are linguistic formulations of *practices*. Practices like these are necessary conditions for us to talk as we do about democracies and dogs. In order to doubt, for example, that there are any democracies left in the world one must *know how* to use the word 'democracy.' There is, however, an important difference between these kinds of hinge propositions, and meta-propositions like: the verification principle, VP, which says that no empirical claim can be accepted unless it can in principle be verified; the principle of contradiction, PC, which says that one cannot allege both p and not p at one and the same time; and the identity principle, IP, which requires us to use the same name for the same object in a specific discourse episode. The scope of these meta-principles, and the practices they formulate is much wider than that of specific definitions and the practices formulated by them. The meta-principles must also be *adhered* to in order for linguistic communication to be even possible—given that human beings are the way they are. If we were all psychic or had a different kind of brain such practices might not be necessary. But we are what we are. Just imagine what it would be like trying to communicate with someone who saw no need for factual confirmation, contradicted himself with great frequency, and never used the same expression to designate the same object. Now imagine a group of such people. They would be unable to take any of the initial steps that language formation requires. Unless our actions are in accordance with principles like VP, PC, and IP, we would not be able to talk at all. They are necessary presuppositions for the very existence of natural languages.[19] In the absence of a practice like the one formulated in the dictionary regarding the word 'democracy,' all that follows is that we would be unable to talk about democracies. One way to mark the difference between the two kinds of hinge propositions I have distinguished would be to distinguish between those which are *hinged to specific topics*, and those that are the *hinges upon which any discussion depends.*

In his book on Moore and Wittgenstein, Stroll explicates what he considers to be Wittgenstein's foundationalism as follows:

> The foundations of language stand *outside of* and yet *support* the language game... These foundations are identified in a series of metaphors as "the hinges on which others turn," "the rock bottom of our convictions," "the substratum of all my inquiring," and most pervasively "that which stands fast for us and for many others" (O. C., 116)... It is Wittgenstein's main thesis in *On Certainty* that what stands fast is not subject to justification, proof, the adducing of evidence or doubt and is neither true nor false. Whatever is subject to these ascriptions belongs to the language game. But certitude is not so subject, and therefore stands outside the language game. It does so in two different forms, one relative, and the other absolute. A proposition that is exempt from doubt in some contexts may become subject to doubt in others, and when it does it plays a role in the language game. This is the relativized form of certitude. But some propositions—that the earth exists, that the earth is very old—are beyond doubt; their certitude is absolute.[20]

It may very well be that Stroll is right about this being Wittgenstein's view. It is not my intention to quarrel over how to interpret Wittgenstein on this matter. The point I want to make is this—Wittgenstein *could* have chosen a different course. He could have argued that those object language assertions within a given language, for example English, that stand fast are to be understood as relative to a particular context of language use, but that those meta-language assertions or formulations, like VP, PC, and IP are absolute in the sense that no human communication would be possible without them. The belief that the earth is very old does not fall into either of my two types of hinge propositions. At one time one might well have doubted this belief. Given what we know today, the belief that the earth is very old is a hinge proposition, but is its certainty absolute? Is not the belief that the earth exists more likely an absolute than the belief that it is very old? It seems clear to me that in more primitive times one might well have reasonably doubted the latter but not the former. In *On Certainty*, Wittgenstein himself claims, regarding the former "...in the entire system of our language-games it belongs to the foundations. The assumption, one might say, forms the basis of action, and therefore, naturally, of thought."[21]

What Stoll takes to be Wittgenstein's "main thesis" in *On Certainty* "that what stands fast is not subject to justification, proof, the adducing of evidence or doubt and is neither true nor false," may well be Wittgenstein's view, but I disagree with it. If I am right, and there are practices that qualify as necessary presuppositions for the very existence of a natural language, that fact itself constitutes a *justification* of them. It would seem to me hard to imagine a stronger or more significant form of justification than this. Hinge statements of the sort I explicated in terms of the "standard metre" kind of case, namely, definitions, both ostensive and otherwise, are as much subject to changing standards as is what constitutes or measures a meter. Wittgenstein himself says, "When language-games change, then there is a change in concepts, and with the concepts the meanings of words change."[22] No single hinge statement of the "standard metre" kind can be said to be justified as being a necessary presupposition for the very existence of a natural language, but VP can. So can PC, IP, and, I suspect, certain others as well. One could, of course, maintain that those practices that are formulated by VP, PC, and IP, since they are necessary for us to even communicate, do *no have to be* justified. But that only means that they do not have to be justified in ordinary or everyday circumstances. It does not mean that they are *never* subject to justification—that there are no circumstances where doing so would be appropriate. Disputes do arise regarding their truth. The dispute between the positivists and the metaphysicians regarding VP is a case in point, and it can be resolved by pointing out that adherence to the practice formulated by VP *is* justified because it *is* a necessary presupposition for the very existence of a natural language.

What is significant about Moore's role in all of this controversy regarding scepticism, certainty, and our knowledge of the external world is that he more than anyone else is responsible for forcing philosophers to face up to the fact that their doctrines are extremely difficult, if not impossible, to reconcile with what we all *somehow* know with certainty to be true. I hope that this chapter and the three preceding it are sufficient evidence to convince the reader of the considerable importance which both his visionary insights and immense analytical skills have played in the present century's clarification and development of these topics.

---

1 Wittgenstein (1972) p. vi^e.
2 Moore (1959) pp. 225-231.
3 Ibid., pp. 231-235.
4 Ibid., p.235.
5 Ibid., pp. 239-241.
6 Ibid., pp. 242-244.
7 Ibid., pp. 248-250.
8 Ibid., p. 250.
9 To be fair, I should point out that according to the editors of this text "Moore was particularly dissatisfied with the last four paragraphs of this paper." p. 251.
10 Ibid., p. 249.
11 Odell (2000) p. 60.
12 See p. 45.
13 Wittgenstein (1972) sect. 481, p. 65^e.
14 Stroll (1994) p. 181.
15 Wittgenstein (1972) sect. 341, p. 44^e.
16 Ibid., sect 115, p. 18^e.
17 Ibid., sect. 50, p. 25^e.
18 It should be noted that this passage answers those who, like George Pitcher, think Wittgenstein must have been mistaken when he claimed, as he did in the passage quoted above about the "standard metre," that "there is one thing of which one can say neither that it is one metre long, nor that it is not one metre long, and that is the standard metre in Paris." Pitcher (1964) p. 182.
19 Odell and Zartman (1982) pp. 72-74.
20 Stroll (1994) p. 138.
21 Wittgenstein (1972) sect. 411, p. 52^e.
22 Ibid., sect. 65, p. 10^e.

8

Moore's Ethics

Moore wrote two books on ethics. The first one, *Principia Ethica*, was published in 1903. The second one, *Ethics*, was published in 1912. In both books he defended the thesis that "goodness" is a non-natural, indefinable, but objective property of things and events in the world.[1] In the preface of *Principia Ethica*, Moore announced his commitment to the analytic method he and Russell pioneered at Cambridge. He alleged that most of the difficulties and disagreements which have characterized ethics, as well all other branches of philosophy, are the direct result of the fact that most philosophers attempt to answer philosophical questions, "without first discovering precisely *what* question it is which" they "desire to answer." He claims that there are two kinds of question that moral philosophers have always been concerned with, but that they "have almost always confused both with one another and with other questions." According to Moore, these two kinds of question are: "What kind of things ought to exist for their own sakes?" and "What kind of actions ought we to perform?"[2]

Like Kant, he is primarily interested in the establishment of a "Prolegomena" to any ethics that can "possibly pretend to be scientific." He says that he has "endeavored to discover what are the fundamental principles of ethical reasoning; and the establishment of these principles, rather than any of the conclusions which may be attained by their use, may be regarded as my main object." He also claims to have attempted to "present some conclusions, with regard to the proper answer of the question 'what is good in itself?'" And, he claims that his answer to this question is "very different from any which have commonly been advocated by philosophers."[3]

Propositions that properly answer Moore's first kind of question are alleged by Moore to be incapable of proof or disproof. He refers to them as "intuitions." Answers to the second kind of question, which he claims are often confused with answers to the first kind, are, in contrast to the first kind, capable of proof and disproof. Since so many judgments that we consider to be ethical judgments concern good or bad conduct, we are apt to think that good and bad conduct is the subject matter of ethics. But, according to Moore, this would be a mistake. There are according to Moore, many *other* things that are said to be good. What we have to discover is what is *common* to *all* of those things, including conduct, that are said correctly to be good. Or to put the matter in different terms, Moore points out that what we seek is a definition of the word 'good.' It is one thing to ask what things are good, another to ask what does the word 'good' mean? This is to utilize the distinction sometimes referred to as the distinction between the *material* mode and the *formal* mode. For Moore, the question in the formal mode is the most fundamental question in ethics. He says:

> That which is meant by 'good' is, in fact, except its converse 'bad,' the *only* simple object of thought which is peculiar to ethics. Its definition is, therefore, the most essential point in the definition of Ethics; and moreover a mistake in regard to it entails a far larger number of erroneous ethical judgments than any other. Unless this first question be fully understood, and its true answer clearly recognized, the rest of Ethics is as good as useless from the point of view of systematic knowledge.[4]

His answer to this question is bound to disappoint us if we expect to be given the usual kind of formal mode response, namely, the word 'good' means such and so. Instead, and paradoxically, we are told that 'good' cannot be defined. Does this mean that the most important question in ethics cannot be answered? Yes and no! He claims that *the* good or that which is good, a substantive, is definable, but that good, an adjective, is not. The good may include other parts. It may involve pleasure, intelligence, etc., as well as good. The question regarding how to define the adjective 'good' cannot, however, be answered by providing a definition in terms of other words. It can only be answered if one recognizes that 'good' like 'yellow' refers to a simple, and not a, complex entity. He tells us the word 'horse,' a substantive, denotes a complex thing and it can be defined by enumerating all of its properties, but when we have reduced our definition of a horse to its simplest terms, these terms cannot themselves be defined. We apprehend goodness, but, according to Moore, we cannot define it. Only complex objects—objects composed of parts can be defined. From this it follows that, for Moore, a word is properly defined only when it is defined in terms of words that designate properties that cannot themselves be defined. Otherwise, the definition would be incomplete.[5]

Philosophers are, according to Moore, prone to misconceive the relation that obtains between goodness and other properties that are associated with it. Philosophers mistakenly assume that those properties that are common features of the good are defining properties of goodness. He says that:

> ...far too many philosophers have thought that when they named those other properties they were actually defining good; that these properties, in fact, were simply not 'other,' but absolutely and entirely the same with goodness. This view I propose to call the 'naturalistic fallacy.'[6]

He proceeds to further explicate and defend this idea by discussing how it manifests itself. Briefly stated, the naturalistic fallacy occurs whenever one attempts to define the good, a non-natural property, in terms of a natural property.[7] An example of this fallacy is, on Moore's account, the hedonistic view that the good *is* pleasure. Moore also claims that this fallacy is committed whenever one defines the word 'beauty' in naturalistic terms,[8] and that Aristotle commits this fallacy when he identifies the good with virtue.[9] Pleasure may well be good, and so may the object of one's desires. The virtues are no doubt good. But none of these things are identical with goodness itself. They simply have the property of being good. If goodness were equivalent to any of these other things, what sense would it make to say of them that they are also good? But then, just what does Moore mean to say when he says that good is a non-natural property of things? His answer seems to be that it is intrinsic property. Good, is an end in itself. It is not a means to something of greater value. For Moore, a virtue is simply a means to the good. A virtue-based approach to ethics is, however, for Moore, superior to hedonism. He says, "inasmuch as virtues are very complex mental facts, there are included in them many things which are good in themselves and good in a much higher degree than pleasure." But the hedonists do have, "the superiority that their method emphasizes the distinction between means and ends," even though they "have not apprehended the distinction clearly enough to perceive that the special ethical predicate, which they assign to pleasure as *not* being a mere means, must also apply to many other things."[10]

But Moore still has not told us precisely what the good is. We do know that for him it is a thing, like yellow, simple and indefinable, but unlike yellow, it is non-natural. Like yellowness, what we actually experience when we experience goodness, cannot be reduced to a material description. Yellowness cannot, according to Moore, be reduced to light vibrations of a specific length. He claims that we "would never have been able to discover" the existence of the light vibrations identified with the various colors, "unless we had first been struck by the patent difference of quality between the different colors." For Moore, the light vibrations associated with yellowness are simply "what corresponds in space to the yellow which we actually perceive."[11]

Unquestionably, one can perceive, and thus know in the sense of "being acquainted with," yellow, and not have any idea that it is definable or analyzable in terms of light vibrations. But this fact in itself is not sufficient to establish Moore's thesis that the one is not identical with or reducible to the other. The prevailing theory of meaning at the time that Moore wrote *Principia* was the *referential theory of meaning*, which maintains that meaning is reference. Moore, Russell, and Wittgenstein were, as I pointed out previously on page 38, united in their adherence to this theory, but because of his efforts to understand and provide an analysis of the concept of identity, the German philosopher Frege rejected it. Frege distinguished between the *sense* (meaning) and the *reference* of denoting expressions. The senses (conceptual meaning) of "The Morning Star" and "The Evening Star" *are* different. The former can be rendered as 'that first bright star that appears in the morning." The latter connotes "that first bright star that appears in the evening." But that fact is perfectly consistent with their references being identical. Likewise, in opposition to Moore, although 'yellow' and 'light vibrations of a specific length' express different concepts, their references may well be identical.

This is not the only problem with Moore's definition. He uses the color word 'yellow' to illustrate what he wants to say about the word 'good.' But there is a considerable difference between a property like yellowness that can be seen, and an alleged property like goodness that cannot. In the literal sense of the word 'see' I can be said to see both the yellowness of a given object, and the light vibrations that are its

73

yellowness. In this sense of the word 'see,' its common or ordinary sense, I see nothing that is an object's goodness. Nor for that matter, do I hear, feel, taste or smell goodness. I know people who I believe are very good people, but this fact about them has nothing to do with my having sensed their goodness, as I sense the yellowness of my favorite shirt. I know people who are warm, loving, forthright, and empathetic about the welfare of other humans, as well as all sentient creatures. And I do describe them as good persons. Sometimes I meet people about whom I immediately *suspect* that they are good persons, but what I mean is that I would be willing to predict that they are loving, forthright, etc. people. Am I wrong to so describe them since my characterization of them is in terms of the *virtues* they possess and not in terms of their possession of the sensible property of goodness? Of course not, 'good person' is simply an abbreviation for a person who possesses virtues, x, y, and z. All that is meant by saying that one senses that a person is a good person is that you sense that that person has certain virtues. To speak of the "goodness" of a person as if it were, somehow, something more than the possession of certain virtues seems to me to introduce not only an indefinable property, but also an unknowable and mysterious one as well. Of what possible use is such an idea?

Good persons understood as virtuous persons, or persons who are "warm, loving, forthright, and empathetic about the welfare of other humans" are not, however, identical with ethical persons. A cold, aloft, unfeeling person, who cares very little about others can be an ethical person in so far as such a person can be someone who can always be counted on to do the right thing. A coldly rational and unfeeling person can, on the basis of commitment to either a consequentialistic, or a Kantian ethic, be a person who predictably follows an ethical course of action. If he is a consequentialist, he may do so because he believes that acting ethically is in his own interest. If he is a Kantian, he may do so for no other reason than that he believes it to be his duty. Moreover, a virtuous person can be someone who often does the wrong thing. Warm, loving, forthright, and empathetic persons are not always intelligent persons. They can be well meaning but characteristically bungling, and as a result do more harm than good. Ethical theories that recognize the overriding importance of conduct over character are referred to in ethics as 'conduct ethics' in contrast to 'virtue ethics.' And some ethicists[12] argue that although virtue ethics is instrumental in the production of right conduct, conduct ethics is logically prior to or presupposed by virtue ethics. Michael Slote (1995) has, however,

74

constructed a compelling case in favor of the contrary view that virtue ethics does not logically presuppose conduct ethics. We need not concern ourselves with this controversy, however, because it is possible to defend the priority of conduct ethics over virtue ethics without making that relationship out to be a matter of logical or conceptual necessity. One can maintain that this priority is simply factual.[13] Specific practices actually perpetuate harmonious coexistence between humans, and an understanding of this fact leads us to encourage and reward those traits of character that promote conduct in accordance with these practices.

Another problem with Moore's account of the good as a non-natural and indefinable property is that he misrepresents the nature of the concept "good" or "goodness." Previously, in Chapter II, I discussed Wittgenstein's notion of "family resemblance." According to Wittgenstein, the word 'good' is a "family resemblance" word.[14] If he is correct about the word 'good' being a family resemblance word or concept, it is pointless to talk about essence, and even worse to conceive of that essence as indefinable. Perhaps, the explanation of Moore's insistence that the 'good' is indefinable lies in the fact that it *is* a family resemblance concept. Given that it is a family resemblance word or concept, it follows that searching for its essence will reveal nothing specifiable to be that essence, and one might confuse this "undiscoverable something" with an "indefinable something."

For Moore, practical ethics, in contrast to theoretical ethics, has to do with the determination of what ought to be done to produce the greatest amount of good in the world. His theory of practical ethics is consequentialistic in nature. He claims that what we are obliged to do, what we ought to do, is determined by the amount of good our actions produce. Early on in *Principia,* Moore claims, "in asserting that the action is *the* best thing to do, we assert that it together with its consequences presents a greater sum of intrinsic value than any possible alternative."[15] He reaffirms this contention later on in the same work, and concludes that it is "demonstrably certain" by arguing that:

> It is plain that when we assert that a certain action is our absolute duty, we are asserting that the performance of that action at that time is unique in respect of value. But no dutiful action can possibly have unique value in the sense that it is the sole thing of value in the world; since in that case, *every* such action would be the *sole* good thing, which is a manifest contradiction... It can,

therefore, be unique only in the sense that the whole world will be better, if it is performed, than if any possible alternatives were taken. And the question whether this is so cannot possibly depend solely on the question of its own intrinsic value... It is, in fact, evident that, however valuable an action may be in itself, yet, owing to its existence, the sum of good in the Universe may conceivably be made less than if some other action, less valuable in itself, had been performed. But to say that this is the case is to say that it would have been better that the action should not have been done; and this again is obviously equivalent to the statement that it ought not to have been done—that it was not what duty required.... Our 'duty' therefore, can only be defined as that action, which will cause more good to exist in the Universe than any possible alternative.[16]

Moore's argument for this conclusion would not have sounded discordant to his contemporaries, but to the well-tuned philosophical ears of today it strikes a false cord. I pointed out a few pages ago that Moore and many of his distinguished contemporaries accepted the referential theory of meaning, which held that the meaning of a term is its reference. On the basis of this idea it is natural to view the meaning of an adjective to be a quality existent in the world. If no such quality exists, then according to this theory the word 'good' would have to be meaningless, but as 'good' is obviously not meaningless, goodness must exist. But if one distinguishes between sense (meaning) and reference, as Frege did, one will not find this inference at all cogent.

According to Alan White, Moore's mistake was in supposing that 'good' is a descriptive word, a word describing a unique characteristic. He says, in opposition to Moore, that the word 'good' "is an *evaluative*, not a purely *descriptive*, word, and hence however complete a description is given of a thing, it always remains to evaluate it."[17] White is right. The word 'good' is quite commonly used to express approval. Moore should not have ignored this fact. It must also be pointed out, however, that when one says of an action that it was a good thing to do, what one is claiming can be taken to mean either that one approves of the action in question, or that it was the *right* thing to do, the *morally obligatory* thing to do. If one means the former, then 'good' is being used in an evaluative sense. But, if it is used to mean the latter, then its use is arguably descriptive, and more importantly, this use is the one of *primary* concern to ethicists. There is nothing paradoxical, odd, or even misleading in saying that although one

76

approves of an action, it is certainly not morally obligatory.

A consequentialist like myself will argue, as I have done, in "Practice Consequentialism: A New Twist on an Old Theory," that moral obligation is a descriptive predicate. On my view of the matter, moral obligation must be understood as a set of practices—practices that exist in the strictest sense of the term 'exist.' Unquestionably, 'good' is often, most often, used to express a value judgment. That is why there is so much disagreement about the value of most things. But how many people really think that one is not morally obligated to tell the truth, or to refrain from harming, killing, or stealing from others? This is not to say, however, that the practices on which these obligations are based are sacrosanct, or that our trusted and reliable commonly held set of moral rules, those that define what I like to call the "Folk Morality," are not subject to revision. Instead:

> There may well be additional rules or different sets of rules which would in themselves or in conjunction with our currently employed set serve to promote the general good more efficiently than it is presently promoted, but all newly contrived rules have to be regarded like *hypotheses* in science. We are, as we are in science, free to hypothesize. We are free to formulate any rule or set of rules we like—an unimpeachable vocation for the ethicist or philosopher. But this freedom is not to be equated with, or misconstrued to be, a freedom to follow or adopt any set we choose. Certain hypothesized practices or rules may appear quite effective in theory, but the real test of their effectiveness is how well they actually do. Unless a practice, rule, or set of practices or rules contributes to or helps bring about harmonious co-existence between humans, it is to be rejected or discarded.[18]

I am not, however, using the term 'hypothesis' in the sense it commonly has in scientific contexts, when I use it to refer to untried ethical principles or practices. As I pointed out in my chapter on Bertrand Russell's ethics in my book, *On Russell*, in the same series as the present work:

> In science when we formulate a hypothesis, we are venturing an explanation for certain observed phenomenon, and having done so, we engage in the construction of experimental contexts, which will confirm or disconfirm our hypothesis. Folk ethics did not develop in parallel fashion. Still, it does make sense to talk about

the empirical consequences of behaving in accordance with a rule or practice. And what is more, one can talk meaningfully about our human history as the experimental context that serves to confirm or disconfirm the effectiveness of various practices, including ethical ones.[19]

My view does not deny that there are cases where one is morally obligated to lie, or even to kill another person. Conventional morality is not a fixed or static morality. We must recognize that moral rules are simply *formulated summaries*—short hand abbreviations—of the *lengthy formulations* which would be required to actually describe the extremely complicated set of prescriptions and prohibitions which comprise our ethical practices. Folk morality does not require that we should *never* lie to, harm, or kill other humans. It requires us only to refrain from doing these things under most conditions. It permits, even condones lying to, or killing other humans under certain specifiable conditions, for example, in defense of one's life, loved ones, home, or country. Our moral rules incorporate these exceptions. "Our rule against killing other humans is inadequately expressed by the biblical abbreviation 'Thou shalt not kill.' Instead it should be abbreviated along the lines of 'Do not kill another human being unless x, y, or z obtain.'"[20]

No doubt, Moore was misled by his commitment to a referential theory of meaning, and he did fail to recognize that the word 'good' is primarily an evaluative and not a descriptive one. Yet, the upshot of the kind of consequentialism I have defended, practice consequentialism, is that he was on the right track when he concluded that practical ethics is primarily a descriptive and not an evaluative discipline. Although we rarely ever use the word 'good' in a descriptive fashion outside the realm of ethics, it is primarily used in ethics to mean objectively good, or as a substitute for 'morally' or 'ethically' obligatory. And, from the perspective of at least one form of consequentialism—practice consequentialism or "folk ethics"—ethics is descriptive of, to repeat part of the quote from Moore on page 77 above, what "will cause more good to exist in the Universe than any possible alternative." For the practice consequentialist, 'good' is defined as "what will promote harmonious co-existence between humans," and the acceptability of moral practices is a descriptive or empirical matter. Our commonplace ethical practices are validated empirically.

Endnotes

[1] See, Sylvester (1990) Chap. I, pp. 3-34.

[2] Moore (1959) pp. vii-viii, 142-147.

[3] Ibid., p. ix.

[4] Ibid., p. 5.

[5] Ibid., pp. 8-10.

[6] Ibid., p. 10.

[7] See, Alan White (1958) pp. 122-127.

[8] Moore (1959) p.201.

[9] Ibid., p. 173.

[10] Ibid., p.173.

[11] Ibid., p.10.

[12] Frankena (1973) pp. 61-67, and Holmes (1993) pp. 79-80.

[13] See, my paper "Practice Consequentialism: A New Twist on an Old Theory" forthcoming, *Utilitas*, vol. 13, 2001.

[14] Wittgenstein (1958) sect. 77, p.36^e.

[15] Moore (1959) p. 25.

[16] Ibid., pp. 147-148.

[17] White (1958) p. 126-127.

[18] Odell (2001) p. 5.

[19] Odell (2000) p. 77.

[20] Odell (2001) p 4.

9

Is Existence a Predicate?

The ontological argument, which originated with St. Anselm, Archbishop of Canterbury, during the eleventh century A. D. in his Proslogium, has had many defenders as well as detractors. Versions of it have been championed by: Duns Scotus, Descartes, Leibniz, Spinoza, Hegel, Karl Barth, Charles Hartshore, and one of Moore's pupils Norman Malcolm. It has was rejected as fallacious at the time of its creation by a monk by the name of Gaunilon. Since then it has had many illustrious critics: St. Thomas Aquinas, Hume, and Immanuel Kant, who argued that it is inherently muddled as regards the nature of existence. According to Kant, it wrongly assumes that existence is a predicate.[1]

Anselm's proof assumes as a first premise that God is perfection, which is to say that he is "that than which nothing greater can be conceived." It proceeds in the form of a *reductio ad absurdum* to conclude that God must exist. A *reductio* argument assumes as a premise the denial of what it wants to prove, and then shows that this assumption is contradictory, and therefore that its denial must be true. If God is truly that than which nothing greater can be conceived, then we cannot deny that he exists without contradicting ourselves. Assume that some thing x is omnipotent (all powerful) omniscient (all knowing, and all seeing) infinitely benevolent, which to assume that x has is God. Now ask, "Can that thing x be God if it does not exist?" According to Anselm to this question in the affirmative is to contradict oneself. Why? Because then I can imagine a y that is omnipotent, omniscient, and altogether benevolent, who in addition also exists. But that means that x is not "that then which nothing greater can be conceived." I am forced to contradict myself.

Kant argued that although the conception of a thing, or subject, does involve its having certain properties, or predicates, existence cannot be one of them. Consider, for example, a unicorn. A unicorn is horse like, is always white, has a twisted conically shaped horn in the center of its forehead, and has magical properties. Consider, further what a perfect racehorse would be. He would always be lameness free, faster than any other horse that has ever, or will ever exist, and altogether gentle and obedient. We had no trouble conceiving of unicorns or perfect racehorses, and we did so without any mention of existence. It is a fact, however, that neither kind of thing has ever existed. No one would be tempted to add that unlike the unicorn we imagined, the perfect racehorse would necessarily have to exist because he is perfect. For this kind of reason Kant concluded that existence is not a property, or a predicate attribute.

Moore addressed the question concerning whether or not existence is a predicate in an essay published in 1936 entitled "Is Existence a Predicate?" And he makes Kant's point in a more perspicuous fashion by applying the method of analysis. He concedes to Frege and Russell, and would concede to Kant, that they are correct in denying that existence is an attribute, in as much as there are uses of 'exists' where the term in question "does not stand for an attribute of an object or individual." Moore argues that although the propositions expressed by 'Some tame tigers growl,' G, and 'Some tame tigers exist,' E, both appear to (he says "appear to" because both 'growl' and 'exist' fill the predicate spot in the same kind of subject/predicate form) attribute properties to tame tigers, there is an important difference. That difference being that although the former proposition *can* be said to assert that there are values of the variable *x* which instantiate two attributes, namely being tame, and being something which growls, the latter *cannot* be said to assert that there are values of the variable x which instantiate two attributes, namely, being tame and being existent. Such an assertion would, Moore argues, be nonsense.[2]

Moore's point is that grammatical form is misleading as to what is implied by G and E. The form of each is the same. They are both of the form "S is P." But, we must not be mislead by this grammatical fact. They are in fact quite different logically. One can claim that "This is a tame tiger, but he does not growl." But one can not say "This is a tame tiger, but he does not exist." To claim the latter would

81

be to claim what is surely a contradiction since to say that this is a tame tiger is to claim that he exists. Moore is not content to let the matter rest here, however. He is not convinced that there are *no* uses of 'exists' where it does stand for an attribute or property of an object. He takes up the case where one would simply say "This exists."

Moore considers the sentence 'This exists,' and argues that in cases where it would be appropriate to say, "This is a tame tiger," it would also be appropriate to point at the object in question and say "This exists," on the grounds that "you can clearly say with truth of any such object, "This might not have existed." Moore cannot understand "how it is possible that 'This might not have existed' should be true, unless 'This does in fact exist' is also true, and therefore that the words 'This exists' [are] significant."[3] His next move is to bring into consideration, as we might predict he would, sense-data.

According to Moore, in every case where one points to an object and says, for example, "This is a tame tiger," one is referring to a sense-datum—one is saying that this sense-datum is *of* a physical object. As we might expect him to do, he argues that any claim that something is a physical object is equivalent to a claim that this sense datum is of a physical object. "This exists," is thus, according to Moore, short for "The thing which this sense-datum is "of" exists." His point is not, of course, of any consolation for those who seek considerations favorable to the ontological argument.

---

[1] By 'predicate' philosophers, including Kant, do not mean 'predicate' in the literal sense, i.e., whatever grammar sanctions as predicable of a subject. In that sense 'existence' is clearly a predicate. What philosophers mean by 'predicate' is an attribute, property, or characteristic, of some subject.

[2] Moore (1959) pp. 117 124.

[3] Ibid., pp.124-125.

SELECTED
BIBLIOGRAPHY

Austin, J. L. (1962) *Sense and Sensibilia* (Oxford: The Clarendon Press)

Broad, C. D. (1958) *The Manchester Guardian*, October 25, 1958, reprinted in Moore (1959A).

Carnap, R (1932) "The Elimination of Metaphysics Through the Logical Analysis of Language," reprinted in *Logical Positivism*, ed. A. J. Ayer (New York: The Free Press, 1959).

Frankena, W. (1973) *Ethics* (Englewood Cliffs, New Jersey: Prentice-Hall Inc.).

Hacker, P. M. S. (1996) *Wittgenstein's Place in Twentieth Century Philosophy* (Oxford: Blackwells).

Holmes, R. (1993) *Basic Moral Philosophy* (Belmont, California: Wadsworth Publishing Company).

James, William (1901-02) *Varieties of Religious Experience*, Modern Library Edition (New York: Random House).

Keynes, John Maynard (1949) *Two Memoirs* (New York: Augustus M. Kelley).

Levy, Paul (1981) *Moore and the Cambridge Apostles* (Oxford: Oxford University Press).

Malcolm, Norman (1963) "George Edward Moore" *Knowledge and Certainty* (Englewood Cliffs, New Jersey: Prentice-Hall, Inc.).

Merrill, John and Odell, S. Jack (1983) *Philosophy and Journalism* (New York & London, Longmans).

Monk, Ray (1996) *Bertrand Russell: The Spirit of Solitude* (New York, The Free Press).

Moore, G. E. (Between 1895-1901) "Art, Morals, and Religion" *The Moore Papers*, Cambridge University Library.

(1947) *Ethics* (London: Oxford University Press).

(1951) *Philosophical Studies* (New York: Routledge & Kegan Paul LTD).

(1953) *Some Main Problems of Philosophy* (London: Allen & Unwin LTD.).

(1959A) *Philosophical Papers* (London: George Allen & Unwin LTD.).

(1959B) *Principia Ethica* (Cambridge: Cambridge University Press).

(1986) *G. E. Moore: The Early Essays*, ed. Tom Regan Philadelphia: Temple University Press).

(1992) *Lectures on Metaphysics*, 1934-1935 ed. Alice Ambrose (New York: Peter Lang Publishing, Inc.).

Odell, S. Jack (2000) *On Russell* (Belmont, California: Wadsworth) (2001) "Practice Consequentialism: A New Twist on an Old Theory" forthcoming, *Utilitas*, Vol. 13, 2001.

(1984A) "On the Possibility of Natural Language Processing," *Theoretical Linguistics*, Vol. II No.1 / 2.

(1984B) "A Paraphrastic Theory of Meaning," *Theoretical Linguistics*, Vol. II No. 3.

(1982) "A Defensible Formulation of the Verification Principle" with James Zartman, *Metaphilosophy*, Vol. 13, No. 1, January 1982.

Pitcher, G. (1964) *The Philosophy of Wittgenstein* (Englewood Cliffs, N. J.: Prentice-Hall, Inc.).

Regan, Tom (1986) *Bloomsbury's Prophet* (Philadelphia: Temple University Press).

Ryle, Gilbert (1963) "Ordinary Language" in *Philosophy and Ordinary Language* ed. Charles Caton (Urbana, University of Illinois Press).

Schilpp, Paul A. (1952) *The Philosophy of G. E. Moore*, The Library of Living Philosophers (New York: Tudor Publishing Company).

Slote, M. (1995) "Agent-Based Virtue Ethics" in *Midwest Studies in Philosophy*, Vol. 20.

Stroll, Avrum (1994) *Moore and Wittgenstein on Certainty* (Oxford: University Press).

Sylvester, Robert P. (1990) *The Moral Philosophy of G. E. Moore* (Philadelphia: Temple University Press).

White, Alan R. (1958) *G. E. Moore: A Critical Exposition* (Oxford: Basil Blackwell).

Wittgenstein, L. (1972) *On Certainty* (New York: Harper Torchbooks, Harper & Row).

(1958) *Philosophical Investigations*, (Englewood Cliffs, New Jersey, Prentice-Hall).